From Sundaes

to

Space Stations

Careers in Civil Engineering

with a Foreword by Celeste Baine

BY REED BROCKMAN

Engineering Education Service Center

Seattle, WA

From Sundaes to Space Stations

Careers in Civil Engineering

by Reed Brockman

Published by:

Engineering Education Service Center (an imprint of Bonamy Publishing)
PO Box 1218
Clinton, WA 98236 U.S.A.
(360) 341-1424
www.engineeringedu.com

Copyright © 2011 by Engineering Education Service Center
Printed in the United States of America

Publishers Cataloging-in-Publication Data
Brockman, Reed
From sundaes to space stations: careers in civil engineering / by Reed Brockman.
p.   cm.

ISBN 13: 978-0-9819300-3-9 (pbk.)

1. Engineering–Vocational guidance–United States   2. Civil Engineering–Vocational
guidance–United States   I. Title. II. Brockman, Reed.

TA157.B66 2011   620'.0023–dc20

How to Order:
Single copies may be ordered from the Engineering Education Service Center,
PO Box 1218, Clinton, WA 98236; telephone (360) 341-1424; Web site: www.
engineeringedu.com. Quantity discounts are also available.

Dedication

Reed dedicates this book to: Rotten Ralphie, who always let me know that work can be fun, and my Zayde, who went to Blueprint School and could fit a PT boat at record speed. This book is also for my mom, who was as far from being an engineer as you can get.

Acknowledgments

I would like to thank Celeste Baine for having the faith in me as I wrote this book. Thanks don't even start to make a dent in the amount of gratitude I have for my wife, Larisa (also a civil engineer). She is patient and understanding as I continually take on more and more public awareness, pre-college outreach and other volunteer projects instead of coming straight home (and deplete our bank account on the way), plus her sketches. As Vinnie and Michelle regularly remind me, she is truly a saint.

While I may be listed as the author of this book, much of its heart and soul was created by the following civil engineers: Bill Kennedy; Brian Brenner; Cari Powers; Carlos Pena; Chan Rogers; Charlie Roberts; Dan Saulnier; David Manugian; David Westerling; Denis Young; John Looney; Katie Saltanowitz; Lisa Freed; Rebecca Ducharme; Rich Matson; Sarah Campbell; Tom Taylor; and Tony Centore. I also want to thank Rick Johansen for his great guidance during college and beyond. Rudyard Kipling, the caveman and the saber tooth tiger also need thanks.

I also want to acknowledge several people deeply entrenched in volunteer efforts to promote STEM education: Michelle Jose, AnaCristina Fragoso and Karen Fung, and the members of the Infrastructure Technical Group of the Boston Society of Civil Engineers; the ASCE Committee on Volunteer Community Service; the ASCE Committee on Pre-College Outreach; Future City and the National Engineers Week Foundation; the Massachusetts Construction Career Days Committee; Gary Spring, Jean Reynolds and Sharon Caulfield for making ThinkFest possible; and Antonio De La Serna for being involved in basically everything. I also want to thank Massachusetts General Hospital for putting me back together.

Of course, I thank Inna, Aaron and Julia, my two brothers, Rob and Jay, plus my dad, the great author and poet Estelle Epstein, my cousin Allie and the bridge inspection crew, especially Vinnie and Greg.

Edited by: Marjorie Roueche

Cover design by: Amy Siddon

Table of Contents

Foreword
by Celeste Baine

Engineers are going to save the world. Period.
The inventions and designs of engineers are
everywhere. Civil engineering is the oldest
engineering discipline and has evolved to include
work:
- helping us get around easier (transportation
  engineering),
- making our environment healthier
  (environmental engineering),
- making sure buildings and other structures
  don't move, even in earthquakes,
  hurricanes, tornados, or tsunamis
  (geological and structural engineering), and
- creating the infrastructure that we use
  every day.

We live in a designed world and engineers are
the practical artists that make it all happen. From
your cell phone to video games to the Internet,
music, and other entertainment, engineers do it
all. On a larger scale, engineers have had a hand
in designing the house you live in, your appliances
(dishwashers, microwaves, refrigerator, heaters
and air conditioners), the roads, buildings, and
utilities.

The field of engineering is so large that this book can only cover a small part of it. You will be amazed at everything that civil engineers can do including working in law offices, going into space, building bridges, designing ice cream shops, and so much more.

As long as there is civilization, there will be civil engineers. You can get in on the cutting edge of making a new world and make the lives of people better by pursuing a civil engineering degree. Not only will you have the satisfaction of doing something important everyday, you will also make a lot of money, and probably have fun along the way too!

I met Reed back in 2005 while on a book tour in Boston. Here was guy that had more energy and passion for helping kids find out about engineering than anyone I had ever met. He was endlessly putting on events, running competitions and talking to teachers. We stayed in touch over the years and because we have the same mission, we work together whenever possible.

I'm honored to share his enthusiasm with you in the pages of this book. If you'll give him a chance, you'll find he has lots of good things to say. He will, no doubt, even change the way you think about engineering.

Introduction

I'm Reed and I'm a Civil Engineer—a profession I wouldn't trade for all the world. This book is a long answer to the question of why.

As we start going to work everyday, even the most special work can start to seem, well, ordinary.

But civil engineering IS exciting in so many ways. I get excited knowing that I help people all the time—I get to see the ideas that were swirling in my head turn into real solutions that I get to see people use. My work is also exciting because I get to go out and play for a while, then I can at other times be in an office, planning, writing and designing. I love that I get to work with others brainstorming ideas, ironing out the best ideas into real solutions, and using the knowledge from the many subjects that I learned in school, as well as some that I learned outside. On some days, my knowledge of canoeing or rope tying[1] can blend with lessons from history class, physics, or other random facts I've crammed into my noggin. Through my work, I sketch, take photographs, write, and talk, and communicate with many people in many different ways. My job gives me a voice, and through it I know that I make a world of difference.

---

1   Reed is actually lousy at knot tying. He is camping right now and really wishes he had better knot tying skills. He tries.

Never mind "Civil," What is "Engineering"?

You hear the word "engineer" used many different ways by so many people that it gets tough for anyone to say what exactly the word means. Is the person with the striped hat driving that train an engineer? Is the person who is always tinkering with the boiler in your school an engineer? What IS this engineering thing? I'll tell you, but first you need to forget what you think an engineer is.

Is your mind a clean slate? Promise? Good.

Some people say that engineering is simply problem solving, but this doesn't quite get at it. Glenda the Good Witch of the North can wave a wand and solve problems, and your mom can solve your coughing problem, but that's not exactly engineering.

Since you are new to this engineering talk, let's lay this out clearly. Engineering is a process for bringing about a difference in the world, and an engineer is a person that leads that process. So, engineering really is a way of thinking; or as a profession, a profession that uses a certain way of thinking.

Engineering As a Way of Thinking

To make this seem real, let's give a run-through of the process of engineering. It all starts with a clear need for an improvement, such as:

- a whole bunch of people in a specific area are getting sick,
- there are huge traffic jams along a popular the roadway, or
- a person with a certain disability requires a new way to use a computer.

All these are needs for improvement. We don't call these problems because it is possible that they are only symptoms of a bigger problem. Let's call them facts. Some facts may not necessarily make people happy, but a good engineer will follow the process to make things better, and not just look for a quick "solution".

For example, a big town in the desert doesn't get enough water, and taking water from neighboring towns makes a quick fix but could wipe them out. Think the big picture. Get the facts. Any change has an effect. Study the whole system. Get to know the people involved. Get to know the laws that would regulate a change. Know enough to be sure that your change is a positive change. There is a solution that will satisfy both the big town and the entire desert community. Find that best solution. This solution needs to be carefully laid out, and this process of presenting well planned solutions in such a way that they can effectively be carried through is the heart and soul of the engineering design process.

The Engineering Design Process

The figure below is one way of looking at the engineering design process. In many schools, the process is shown as Steps 1-8 without the extra loops. This figure basically follows what I've experienced in the real world.

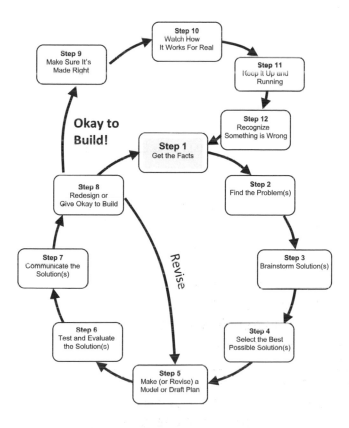

Figure 1-The Engineering Design Process

Engineering Step 1: Get The Facts

Engineers understand that they need all of the facts in one place, and so they often lead the effort to get the full picture of a situation. Here is an example from the world of public health: a group of people are getting sick somewhere. Engineers would collect all the medical data, including a map of where each sick person lives, air and water quality information, where and what they ate, worked, or went to school.

If there are problematic traffic jams, engineers will need data on where each car comes from. They could count cars at intersections or measure the widths of the roads, figure out if the sun is bothering the drivers, or if something else is blocking the view of drivers and interrupting traffic flow.

How about helping people in need on a personal level? Say there is a person unable to operate a computer because of a physical disability. An engineer could figure out how much force his or her muscles can exert, or how much head flexibility he or she has, and collect information about the easiest way for that person to access the keyboard or mouse.

> The first step in engineering is to get the facts. From the collection of facts, engineers can figure out the problem.

Engineering Step 2: Find The Problem(s)

An engineer probably doesn't sound that different from an investigator, because they aren't. Just as crime scene investigators measure and collect from every inch of a crime scene, an engineer figures and measures everything around about the problem, or in many cases problems. Just as a CSI investigates crimes, an engineer investigates problems. But a CSI is done once the crime is solved. An engineer may have found several problems that can be solved, but the solutions are not likely to be ready. When everyone is confident that the list of problems to solve is complete, the collected facts are used in one of my favorite steps—brainstorming a solution.

> The second step in engineering is to figure out the problem. To find a great solution, we must understand the real problem, which is not always obvious.

Engineering Step 3: Brainstorming

Brainstorming is popular among many in the profession, and I know it may even strike a heartwarming chord with some still in school. During brainstorming, everyone involved focuses on making a list of ideas. What is needed at this stage is good solid teamwork.

To be a good team there can be:
- No judging, and
- No arguing.

The number one ingredient needed at this stage is just some good solid teamwork. Let your imagination run wild. If someone thinks an idea will not work, tell them to save their comments for later and work as a team to keep the brainstorming momentum moving forward.

I volunteer as the New England Regional Coordinator for the Future City Competition, which is a daunting task but one that brings great satisfaction. What do I love about it? I get to see brainstorming at its best. I get to see students in grades 6 through 8 let their minds go wild and develop the city of their dreams. For more detail, go to www.futurecity.org.

The goal is to develop a city, including the countless systems that make it function including transportation, energy, water, waste, and safety. Each team starts fresh to develop what they wish, and by the end of the competition, to tie their seemingly way-out ideas to realistic technology and engineering. By letting ideas flow freely during brainstorming and not dismissing crazy sounding ideas, the teams come up with amazing concepts year after year. Often I see ideas that not only have I not envisioned, but that cause me to stop and say "Hmm, a city powered by bees? Is it possible? Real-life avatars? Flying robodoctors that respond to emergencies? Underwater domed cities on fault lines?" I've seen a lot of great ideas come out of this competition. Are they feasible? At this point, nobody knows, but I say: Turn the imagination faucets on full, let the thoughts flow freely, and get a big bucket ready to catch them all!

Remember, there's no limit to brainstorming. If the problem is vacuuming dust out of hard to reach places in a room, the idea of eliminating hard-to-reach places is as valid as ideas for developing a robotic vacuum—at least at this stage. Having a team is a good idea, and the best brainstorming sessions come from having a diverse team working together.

If creating a fun toy for children with a certain disability, the input from the child on how to solve the problem will be different from the input and ideas from a toy company's engineer, physical therapist, parent, or teacher. Also, with a word like "fun" stated in the problem, it might be hard to get agreement from a group of children, even if they all have the same disability. Diversity is the spice of life, and freedom in an open brainstorming session is where the real beauty of the diversity of ideas and experiences can be seen.

> The third step in engineering is to brainstorm possible solutions to the problem chosen. Be sure to brainstorm enough solutions to be sure that, once you weigh the pros and cons in the next step, you will be satisfied with a solution from the list. There is no law against revisiting this step at any time!

Engineering Step 4: Picking The Best Ideas

We can't stay in dreamland, or in a high-flying brainstorming session, forever. To move forward, the pros or "plusses," and cons or "minuses" are weighed out for each idea that was raised. As you have probably learned, it is best to get things right the first time, and good engineers know better than to rush this step. As engineers start eliminating bad ideas and keeping good ones, they can find the best solutions and then look for feedback. If most people involved think a solution is a good idea, then the group can start getting into the nitty-gritty details of the solutions.

This step, picking the best ideas, involves putting values on the facts you gathered. Which facts are important? Is there a clear objective? A good engineer is able to step into the shoes of the people who will use the design, and picture any scenarios that might come. The goal is to make sure things are improved. If something is ruined as a result of change, or if the design is too costly or not durable enough, it is not a great design. Like Goldilocks and the three little bears, an engineer aims to get things "just right!"

This is what many people think of as the entire process, but the whole design process has much more to it.

The fourth step in engineering is to pick the best solution for a final design. This conceptual solution should not get too involved in details, but needs to cover all the needs well enough that an effective final, detailed design can be created.

Engineering Steps 5-8: The Main Event

Steps 5 through 8 include the guts of the design. Physical and computer models are made. Calculations, details, and directions on how to make things (what we call specifications) are developed during these steps as well as estimating costs.

From time to time during this process, you and your design team should look for feedback and improve your design if you can. Remember, if there is critical feedback and your design misses on making real improvement, it is not too late to go back to the drawing board and start the process over again.

The process of design has many steps that loop upon themselves:
- make a model or draft plan,
- test it out or check it over,
- communicate what you've come up with, and
- either go for making the real thing, or
- go back to the drawing board and make needed improvements.

It's worthwhile to go through several loops and get all the feedback you can. After you pick the best ideas, you have a clear idea of what you want, but you don't have any real details.

Often in civil engineering, we begin figuring out details with a computer model or drawings. Using computations (math) and the drawings or models to figure out how each part should be made. When designing software, engineers often go straight to creating an early version of the software and testing it out to make improvements. In the mechanical engineering world, computer simulations or simplified versions of the real product are made. No matter how we go about modeling a final solution, we are trying to envision what we are making to guarantee that everything works. It is very unusual to get perfect results on the first try.

However, the goal of an engineer is to find and communicate solutions, and at some point, planning must stop to create the real thing, no matter what that "real thing" may be. Engineers oversee this process and make sure that their ideas are carried through and the final product works.

> The fifth through eighth steps in engineering are hashing out a design aimed at achieving the intended solution. These steps need plenty of feedback and can be repeated as many times as necessary to be sure it will work well.

In the next steps, someone is taking the words and drawings of the engineer as a set of instructions and translates exactly what the engineer has specified into reality (or discusses the matter with the engineer and creates the agreed upon alternative).

Engineering Steps 9-12: The Real Thing

In steps 9-12, the manufacturing or construction worlds take the front seat, while engineers simply make sure that their ideas are being brought about as intended.

Everybody has heard a story at some point of people making three wishes, and the wishes not turning out as planned. It is the responsibility of engineers to make sure this does not happen. Every effort was made in Steps 1-8 to be sure that their intended solution is clearly described to the degree that others can make it real, but it cannot ever be expected that there will be no questions, misinterpretations or just plain mistakes. Using the utmost in diplomacy and logic, engineers have to work with others to resolve any issue that could prevent the project from achieving its goal.

The job of an engineer should never end as soon as the project is either constructed or manufactured. Engineers look for improvements. If a bridge is built and an engineer sees a problem, it must be fixed—especially if public safety is at risk. The modifications and fixes go through the same design process: gather facts, brainstorm solutions, find a solution, design it while gathering feedback, and adjust as needed.

Engineers rarely "make" anything. We communicate how to do things, but are usually not the people assembling the final product.

The next big step in the process is to make sure ideas can be translated into reality. Art, craft, and communication skills (including grammar, penmanship, spelling, and all the presentations you have given in class) really pay off here. The best solution in the world becomes worthless if it can't be understood by those putting it all together.

Even after a new product or solution is in use, it needs to be periodically reviewed to see how it is working and if there is a need for improvements. The world changes, parts grow old, and the needs of people change as well. For example, if you designed a car with the steering wheel on the right side, and then people started driving on the right side of the road, it would be time to redesign the car with the steering wheel on the left.

Sometimes you can get away with a small change or modification (which we call a retrofit), but other times you need to go back to scratch (which we call a redesign or a replacement.) Are things making sense? The design process is all about solving a problem using the whole bag of tricks you have learned. It may involve math and science, or an understanding of history or local culture. You may need to know local rules or tastes just as much as you need to know the strength of a material.

The ninth through twelfth steps in the engineering design process are to help your design properly translate into a real product—be it a car, a bridge or a bowling ball. These steps also involve keeping an eye on the finished product after it is in use, making sure it is properly functioning as a solution to the problem.

Conclusion

For engineers, there is a method to designing: a step-by-step process that has developed over time. Although this method is called "the engineering design process" it is a very useful tool regardless of the profession you pursue. This method helps you think more effectively, and law, medical, and business schools respect this training. For that reason, many engineering students go on to become attorneys, doctors and business people.

If you were to become an engineer, no matter what kind of engineering you do, your work most likely will follow this design process, or you are performing work that covers a few steps of a bigger process, with others performing the other steps.

While knowing this process is good training for an engineer, having skills to use it is not quite enough for people to call themselves engineers. An engineer is someone who pursues the profession of designing, hopefully following the engineering design process. In the next section we will discuss the work of actual engineers.

Engineering as a Profession

Let's play a game. Read the description of someone's line of work, and guess which of the following are engineers:

    a. "I drive a train."
    b. "I maintain a building."
    c. "I build bridges."
    d. "I design beautiful buildings."

The "I drive a train" person (a) is an engineer, but in a different sense of the word. This other meaning of the word drives some engineers nuts, so remember, if you want to annoy engineers, ask them about their trains. While engineers (the ones discussed in this book) do design train cars, engines, tracks, and signals, if he or she is driving a train, it is a second job or hobby.

The "I maintain a building" person (b) is an engineer by our meaning if he or she observes problems with a facility, thinks up corrective measures, design them, and communicates the solutions. Sometimes these engineers carry out the solutions themselves. If his or her tasks are limited to unblocking toilets or mopping floors, he or she is not performing engineering tasks and should not be calling themselves one.

The person responding "I build bridges" (c) needs to be asked a few more questions. This profession could be the work of a contractor, anybody in the construction trade, an assembly line worker, a craftsman, or one of a large number of professions, but not, at least by definition, the work of an engineer. An engineer may actually make the end product, but that would be taking on an additional job. If he or she uses the design process, and the expertise developed through learning the process, then he or she is an engineer.

In the world of bridges, an engineer is involved in every stage of a bridge's life. First, engineers help figure out where a bridge should go, then they figure out the exact materials and the best way to put them together. Engineers make sure that contractors put bridge pieces together the right way and solve any questions that arise while it is being built. Engineers make sure the bridge is safe after it is built, and they design any needed repairs throughout the life of the bridge. It is usually an engineer who makes the decision that a bridge needs to be closed or replaced.

The "I design beautiful buildings" person (d) could be either an engineer or an architect. The type of engineer who does this work either calls themselves an architectural engineer or a structural engineer. The difference between architectural and structural engineers and architects has long been debated. If licensed, either can design buildings.

Architectural and structural engineering and architecture may seem like the same profession; but oddly, the two groups sometimes clash with one another. An architect is an artist whose goal is to create spaces and places. Many architectural

and structural engineers consider their job to be
to translate an architect's ideas into real plans and
specifications. If the design process is divided so
that the creative process is left to one person and
the technical work is done by another, the two
people must understand and respect the work of
the other. Teamwork is of the utmost importance,
and a great structural engineer understands
architecture as a great architect understands
structural engineering.

Becoming a Professional Engineer

With the title "engineer" comes a large
responsibility. Engineers create plans to solve
problems and instruct others on bringing about
needed changes. While this may sound a little
intimidating, think about it: you can dream it up
and see it come to life, which is very serious, yet
very cool.

In certain types of engineering, the safety of
the public is in the hands of the engineer and a
license is required. A license gives you the title
of "professional engineer" and you can add the
letters "P.E." to the end of your name. I'm a P.E.
because I design, inspect and maintain bridges.
Check out the cover of this book to see how it
looks. Can you imagine the letters P.E. behind
your name?

To get a license, you need to apply and pass an
exam after you prove that you have years of

experience as a junior engineer and show samples of your work.

In some fields of engineering, there is less emphasis on licensure than in others. But in fields directly affecting the public, the title "P.E." is often needed. In many fields of engineering, long debates over who has the right to call themselves an engineer have happened because, if misunderstood, someone could seem to have expertise they don't really have.

Learning From Each Other

When you first start out working as an engineer, senior engineers mentor you by checking your work, encouraging, and teaching you. In the working world, you don't generally use college textbooks nor study day and night. The senior engineers will guide you, but you may need to study up on something you learned in college every once and awhile. When you begin working in engineering, you get real-world knowledge and can see how EVERYTHING you learned is useful, from 4th grade arts and crafts to middle-school geography to that "History of the 60's" course you took as a college elective. Coworkers and managers share their knowledge and you can start building up your "bag of tricks."

If you become an engineer, enjoy the early days and learn all you can. After a while, you will become one of those folks happy to share your knowledge, give guidance, and be ready to take on more responsibility.

Scientists, Engineers, and Inventors

People regularly mix up the words scientist, engineer, and inventor. What exactly is the difference? What does each really do?

An engineer solves problems by delving into his or her "bag of tricks" and figuring out how to make real solutions. Scientists discover by collecting data and seeking patterns. Scientists often play a big part in the initial steps of the design process. If there are data about the environmental conditions related to a disease, a scientist would figure out the pattern and what is happening biologically.

In the beginning, engineers looks to scientists to research a problem, and scientists look to engineers to design equipment to help in this research. Scientists play a large part in the "main event" of the design process. For example, an engineer uses a formula to understand all of the factors in a design, which would not be possible if a scientist had not researched or discovered the formula. Of course, a person can be both a scientist and engineer but more often than not, the two are separate.

By definition, an inventor develops something that has never been seen before. Inventions are designed, and so inventors have done the work of an engineer, whether they call themselves that or not. Inventing often involves a lot of research, and so they are also performing the work of a scientist. We need to be careful not to get too bogged down in this talk—describing the work of a person with a single word or phrase can belittle the efforts of the person. Remember that scientists often design, engineers often invent, and inventors often research.

One example of a person whose work cannot be summarized with a simple description is Amy Smith, whom I consider a true hero. Amy works through the Massachusetts Institute of Technology (MIT) and calls her brand of engineering "appropriate design." She, along with groups of students, visit places around the globe and observe people's practices, resources, culture, and any things that make daily life difficult. She and her team work closely with the community to find solutions that are cost-effective, easily made with local resources, and most importantly, make an improvement that people are excited about. Engineer, scientist, educator, inventor, humanitarian, hero—these words together begin to describe her, but no one word alone would do her justice.

To sum up, engineers figure out solutions to problems and communicate those solutions to those that will carry out their designs. They use not only math and science, but everything they know or have researched through the course of their design in developing the solution to that problem. They use their verbal, written, drawing and all other communication skills in the process of transferring these solutions from their minds to the minds of those who will make their intended solution a reality. It is only on a rare occasion that an engineer, at least the sort of engineer intended in this book, drives a train.

Then What is "Civil" Engineering?

Simply put, civil engineers do the work that keeps society flowing. If a coast is eroding away, civil engineers figure out ways to keep it from washing out neighborhoods. If there is bad drinking water, civil engineers figure out the best way to make it clean and healthy. Sanitation problems? Bad air? Traffic problems? Civil engineers are there.

There is a favored word in the civil engineering world: infrastructure, which means "the built environment". But what's that? Get ready for a story.

Once upon a time, in the age of prehistory, people used to spend much of their time being chased by saber-toothed tigers or hunting little critters. When there were trees and bushes in the way, they realized they would be eaten less if they cleared the path and could run faster. This was the beginning of a built environment: a path. Humans started to change the natural world to better their lives. And then there were all the rivers. Just imagine running from a humongous fanged cat and finding a river in your way. Then one day a woolly mammoth knocks over a tree and you can get to the other side. Someone must have thought a path should go right to this log. Then eventually, someone must have thought of putting the logs where They would be useful. The built environment grows as bridges entered the infrastructure. The idea of making better shelters must have also occurred to our ancestors making rocks and logs really useful for making better roads, better caves, better bridges, and more and more infrastructure.

After they figured out they could plant seeds and crops, people didn't need to run so far for their food. They started trying to protect what they had, which some people believe was the start of real civilization: settled communities as opposed to random running around.

Jump through time to now with our lights, phones, wireless Internet, and subways (I'm in one now as I write–blessed modern technology.) As long as society wants more infrastructures, gadgets and gismos, there will be jobs for engineers.

Infrastructure (built environment):Good;

Sharp-toothed tiger: Bad.

The Wide, Wide World of Civil Engineering

Civil engineering involves our built environment.

Infrastructure is anything we build that is part of our environment, and how we crazy humans collect stuff, protect ourselves, fuel up, or deposit waste. Tunnels, pipes, mines, and shafts poke through the planet in various directions, and we have also buried many utility conduits, pipes, and cables. Actually, the bottom of most of the structures stick into the planet's surface at least a little.

Now let's move onto the earth's surface. Imagine that the world is made up of places, connections between places, and things that make places work. For the most part, the surface of the earth is either water or land (or some mix of both).

1. Water: The people that live and work on the water part of the world can be supported by simpler infrastructure. The places that need more built structures are underwater places and offshore drill rigs. Compared to the number of people who live in cities and towns on the land part of the earth's surface, very few need structures built on the oceans to support them.

2. Land: Every person who lives on land uses the water to connect between places, We also build canals, underwater tunnels, or

bridges to connect land on either side of the water. On occasions, civil enqineers solve unique problems with unique solution such as the bridge built to carry one river over another in Magdeburg, Germany.

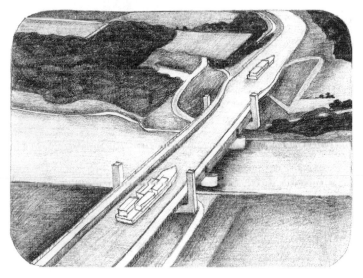

Figure 2 - Yes, this is a RIVER over a RIVER!

We build near shorelines to protect communities from the natural hazards that come from the sea. We build wharves, dams, seawalls, causeways, bridges, culverts, tunnels, jetties, dikes and many other structures to get around at the water's edge without falling in. And those beautiful beaches we love so much? Many wouldn't be half as beautiful without the tender loving care and efforts of a civil engineer.

And finally, about the infrastructure that you see above the ground on terra firma. There are skyscrapers, homes, businesses, and roads connecting them. Utilities are strung over the land—sewer pipes, electric cables, and towers. The more buildings there are, the more roads and utilities are needed to support the people who live and work there.

But, much of what mankind has created on this planet cannot be detected by simply looking. These are the systems that have been created in countries all over the world to control things or share information. Roads and other transportation systems (planes, boats, trains, you name it) have many systems that keep traffic in control, let people know of emergencies, and generally keep things safe and flowing.

Humans have built all sorts of systems to manage pollution and keep it from harming us. Most people wouldn't even know the systems were there if not pointed out. In the past hundred years, we have developed systems to share information wirelessly, making infrastructures all but invisible.

Look up in the sky. More and more, we are building up there, putting up satellites and space stations and continuing the quest away from our planet.

If the planet is not doing something for itself and humankind feels the need to work with the planet and make a little alteration, there's a civil engineer involved in it.

So you may be thinking to yourself that civil engineers do everything. We do a whole bunch, but our projects usually tie into many other branches of engineering as well. A civil engineer may work out the signal timings for a traffic intersection, but it takes an electrical engineer to work out the circuitry. A civil engineer may design a tunnel, but it takes a mechanical engineer to make sure that healthy air pumps throughout. While a civil engineer may design a facility for treating sewage, chemical engineers design the treatment process. This is another one of the beautiful aspects of civil engineering—there are so many opportunities to work with other types of engineers. Depending on the project, you can learn so much about how things work just by working with so many others.

When I was a student, I was assigned to monitor reconstruction of a birdhouse in the Philadelphia Zoo. Although the project was considered a structural engineering effort, I was amazed watching the mechanical contractors install the piping system needed for a tropical environment into an artificial rock mountain. The civil engineering world can involve any other form of engineering, from nanotechnology to computers to mechanical to chemical.

Adding to the amazing diversity of civil engineering is the fact that every civil engineer can specialize in a part of a project. You can be a computer modeler, or a civil engineer that specializes in the initial planning phase of a project, or someone who inspects existing civil engineering creations to make sure they are working.

The rest of this book discusses the primary professions that civil engineers pursue, but it is far from a complete list. We will visit the worlds of civil engineers who:

- make sure things stay strong and stay put,
- design things to move along nicely,
- design places people like,
- design to keep the environment clean,
- design infrastructure to work with all the flowing water on this planet, and
- design places in space.

Designing to Make Sure Things Stay Strong and Stay Put: Geotechnical and Structural Engineers

Remember the poor guy running away from the tigers? If he had a good solid house, he would have stood a better chance. A good, solid house needs to do far more than just hold back a tiger, however. It needs to keep out water. It needs to resist wind and maybe even survive earthquakes. A good house needs to be both held down and able to keep from sinking into the earth.

The things mentioned above are what we call forces, and designing structures that can withstand these forces is one of the main goals of geotechnical and structural engineers. One of these forces is the weight of whatever we build, called a "dead load". A funny name, but they really just call it that because it isn't going anywhere. That saber-toothed tiger we were talking about? That's a live load.

Dead and live loads are the two most talked about loads in the life of a structural engineer. If you are designing a library, you can estimate dead load because you roughly know where the bookcases will be and how tall they are, you can estimate how much they will weigh. Engineers usually pump up the number to be safe.

Live loads are harder to know so precisely. Live loads are any loads you can imagine putting force on a structure after it has been built. Engineers need to add an extra safety factor in structural calculations because you never quite know what loads might happen in the future. People have laid out guidelines for picking these weights, and a whole bunch of other loads we worry about as well.

I remember I was once asked to help redesign a portion of an apartment building. The live loads normal for an apartment floor are at most fifty pounds for every square foot. I was asked to recheck the design for one of the top floors being used as a floor-to-ceiling aquarium. Water weighs 64 pounds a square foot and if the tanks are ten feet tall, there is a live load of 640 pounds per square foot. This is much, much bigger than that original fifty pounds. Without adding extra support for the weight, something may go ba-woosh! Poor folks downstairs!

> **Dead Load**—The weight of whatever we need to build.
> **Live Load**—Any weight that puts force on a structure after it is built.

The earth itself and the water on and in it bring in a whole other group of forces, including snow, wind and earthquake forces, which brings us into the world of the geotechnical engineer. The word "geotechnical" means "the behavior of earth's materials," which include:

- rocks,
- clays,
- silts,
- sands,
- water,
- big cavernous holes,
- lava, and so many other things.

The materials that make up this swirly, wet, blue rock, can behave differently depending on their temperature, how deep in the ground they are, or even because of other materials near them.

The ground does all sorts of funky things, really. Having soft and mucky areas is a problem you must have seen on your shoes at one time or another. Sometimes the ground is so cold or compacted solid that it is tough to build anything in it. And of course, sometimes the ground can just move like during an earthquake. Geotechnical engineers know the ground and know how to work with it.

I love watching geotechnical engineers work. They find out what others discovered when they were working nearby. They pound a hollow pipe

called a "split spoon sampler" into the ground
with a big hammer, counting how many "blows"
it takes to pound it into the ground a foot.
Because they can't test everywhere, they use
their best judgment to figure out what makes
up the ground between test spots. It's half high
tech and half pure simplicity—half technical and
half art. You see, usually there is no way to truly
know what goes on everywhere under the ground.
If geotechnical engineers know less about the
ground; they are more careful and perhaps those
walls won't be so high or that building so tall.

Geotechnical engineers must make sure things
don't sink too deep into the ground[2]. Engineers can
prevent this in several ingenious ways, including:

- spreading out the weight of a structure over
  a big area,

- sticking a long pipe, known as a "pile" or
  "drilled shaft", deep into the ground far
  enough that it hits solid rock, or

- putting parts of it deep enough that there
  is plenty of earth pressing against the sides
  and keeping it from settling in further.

All of these parts of the structure, which are there
to keep it from settling into the earth are called
foundations—many technical folks also call them
substructures, which makes sense when you look
at the word. It is the bottom (sub) part of the
structure holding up the load of the rest.

---

2   It may sound weird, but things in the ground can also float
up. The forces that do this are buoyant forces (see the word "buoy"
in there? It means "float".) Sometimes they make structures extra
heavy just to keep this from happening.

Geotechnical engineers also figure out things you can do to the earth around the structure to help the structure stay still. Sometimes they beat on the ground to get out all the fluff, making it dense and packed tight. Sometimes they pump the water out of the soil to make it less squishy[3]. Sometimes they mix or inject strong materials like concrete into the soil to give it more strength.

So geotechnical engineers make sure the ground can handle what is built. Meanwhile, structural engineers design what is being built. The two make a natural team—the structural engineer cannot design without knowing that the ground will stay put, or that the structure has enough of a grip on the earth it sits on.

From the base up, the structural engineer figures out the nitty-gritty of a design, figuring out how strong every piece of a structure needs to be and how all the parts will come together. The structural engineer knows how the forces and the elements will affect the structure and can select just the right materials to put together in just the right way to work.

The work of a structural engineer is to keep a structure from moving too much, and even more importantly, making certain that parts will not break.

Forces affect every piece of a structure and any given piece will either bend, twist, shear off, be stretched, or get squished.

3   Not a technical term.

Stretch

Okay, you are running away from a saber-toothed tiger and climb up a vine. The vine pulls straight and is in tension, and you are probably feeling some tension too. After all, there is only so much tension that vine can take, and in your panicked rush, you didn't exactly have time to calculate that number. While climbing, the strength of the vine pops in your head. Can it handle your weight? If the tiger gets the rope (as it is trying to do), you are pretty sure it will snap, but will it snap near the top or just above the tiger below? You really start feeling hopeless as you realize that there is more tension in the rope above you because that rope holds both you and the tiger, and to add just a little more misery— your trajectory when falling will probably be right into those gnashing jaws.

Finally, when you climb up to the branch above. You feel great being no longer in tension. What you don't realize is that the cat is happy also. He could neither climb up nor down that rope, but he can walk right up the tree. Aren't you glad that we people developed enough tools and eventually, enough infrastructure to avoid these problems?

Squish

Another day, you see a big coconut far overhead. Not having invented a ladder yet, you get your neighbors together. Your plan is to have everyone climb on each others' shoulders, making a big human tower to grab the coconut. You near the coconut, just a few more inches, but everyone under you is screaming that they are getting squished (especially that little guy down on the bottom). You explain to them that "squished" is not a very technical word and that they should be saying that they are in "compression". Their grumbles get much louder. You think that when you get that coconut and your feet are back on the ground, you better be very nice to them and share that coconut, because they have clubs and can put you through some serious compression. Compression means "squished".

Bend, Twist, and Shear

Think about a whole bunch of cave people on a log, learning how important it can be to go one at a time. Picture crocodiles in the river looking up at them with jaws wide open. As each person climbs onto the log, the wood creaks and bends nearer to the water. As the crocodiles lick their chops, it dawns on them: the ends of this log aren't going anywhere. It goes across the water, with both ends sitting on dry ground (this area of the logs on the ground are known as the "bearing area"). But, when they all walk towards the middle of the log, it bends.

When they all run to one end, the end of the log makes cracking sounds like there is too much load. If they don't spread out a little, that end might either get crushed or snap off (which is known as "shearing"), causing the log to drop off its end support.

The end of their short story, unfortunately, comes when they climb out onto the limbs coming out of the log. This causes that log to spin, twisting and spinning into the river. Chomp! This twist force is torsion, and a log just thrown across a river usually can't handle that kind of force.

There is more involved in how structural engineers think about materials, but the three major ones are:
1. Bending—the effect of the big load in the middle of the log,
2. Shear—the effect of the big load at the end of the log, crushing the end, and
3. Torsion—the off-centered force that spun the log.

Along with compression, and tension.

At this point, let's meet some structural engineers. They use some technical words, but don't run away, if you stick with it, you'll learn about some very cool projects.

In the Shop: Brian Brenner

Brian Brenner, a Structural Engineer at a company called Fay, Spofford & Thorndike (and the gifted, funny author of *Bridginess and You Can't Throw This Away!*), writes about bridge inspection and structural health monitoring.

Making sure bridges are safe has always been important. For decades, engineers have inspected bridges. In the US, bridges must be inspected every two years by law. In special cases, structures may be inspected more frequently.

Over time, and with the help of scientists and research, the methods of bridge inspection have improved, taking advantage of new technologies. But the basic approach remains the same: engineers visit a bridge and carefully observe and document parts of the structure. Engineers

look for corrosion and signs of weakness. For example, steel girders may show signs of rusting and loss of section, which means that part of the steel is corroded. Concrete slabs and walls may be cracked. If enough damage is found, they will restrict access to the bridge, or even close it.

You may have noticed signs when driving over a bridge listing weight limits for trucks. These signs were the result of "load ratings". When engineers inspected the bridge, they did a study on how much weight it could support, and then recommended posting a sign showing the limit and keeping the heaviest trucks off of the bridge.

In the near future, the bridge inspection process may be better with Structural Health Monitoring (SHM). SHM uses computers, databases, the Internet, sensors and new technologies to analyze the health the decades-old bridges. SHM measures and models the movements of a bridge (or part of a bridge), and then compare the results to what is expected. For example, when a bridge beam is carrying a certain weight, the amount it will "deflect" or drop down, can be calculated by a load equation. If a steel beam has rusted, deflections are greater than for an uncorroded beam, say 2 inches instead of the calculated 1 inch. This increased deflection (bending) is a clue that something not good is happening with the structure.

By measuring the structural performance of the bridge under loading, and comparing the measurements to what is expected, it is possible to determine where problem areas are developing on the bridge with time. In the past, engineers didn't have access to the excellent new tools provided by today's technologies. SHM systems will be increasingly feasible in the future because analysis methods have improved, instruments to measure the structure have improved, and data can be organized and remotely reported by the Internet wirelessly. So, not only will engineers go out to physically inspect bridges, but they will be able to turn on their computers each day and get a report on how the bridge is doing.

While the basic idea for SHM is simple, applying it is complex and still the subject of scientific research. Engineering professors are very active at universities around the world developing prototype (model) systems in the laboratory and on actual bridges. Eventually, once the research is a success, maintenance and repair of bridges will be greatly aided by SHM bridge systems.

-Brian Brenner

Advancements in bridge inspecting is just one of the many things that a structural engineer could do. Brian is "tech talking" here, which can be intimidating to those not used to engineering terms, but read it over. Structural engineers often talk about basic physics: there is always some object, such as a bridge, that is subjected to loads (its own weight, truck loads, snow or ice, etc.). Over time, structures and the materials that make up a structure change. If parts are acting strange Brian thinks about gizmos that can help us figure this out.

In the Shop: Tony Centore

Tony Centore is recently retired but was one of the foremost structural engineers in the Boston area for years. He writes this about a bridge reconstruction project.

One of my early assignments was the reconstruction of a highway bridge over a small river in a large urban city. The Agency in charge of the project was very involved in parks and recreation and stressed to the design team that aesthetics (looks) and retention of certain features of the existing single span bridge was a key element of the design project. The existing bridge built in the 1920's was a single concrete span of arched beams. The view of the bridge from the adjacent park land was very dramatic and really fit in with its environment. Replicating the exterior (often the "fascia", which is the part of the bridge you would see if you looked at it from the sides)

concrete beams with a curved soffit (soffit means "underside") proved to be an expensive process.

Our design team did some brainstorming on possible cost-effective solutions. Because the bridge underside was close to the river level, passers by only got a view of the bridge's exterior girders. The interior girders were hidden from view. The design team came up with the idea of using conventional steel wide flange sections (this just means the good ol' steel beams you always see that look like the letter "I") made composite with a concrete deck ("composite" just means that they are physically attached to each other—there are welded little pieces sticking off the steel beams that grab onto the concrete when it hardens, so if the beam wants to bend, the concrete gets pulled with it). Unpainted steel was chosen for the interior girders and a precast concrete beam with curved soffit was selected for the exterior or fascia girders.

The challenging aspect was the exterior concrete girders (the interior girders are ordinary and can be easily shipped and built, but these exterior girders were very heavy and had a fragile shape because they are skinny in the middle where you most need the strength). Building forms on-site for these beams would be complicated, costly, and negatively impact the river below. The design team consulted with a precast concrete producer. The concrete producers indicated they could build a concrete beam with a curved underside that could support its own dead weight and be *transported over the road without problem.*

All seemed to be resolved except when we started to look at how these exterior beams were going to be erected and transported. The precast exterior beams were basically long and narrow. We were concerned with deformation (which means its shape changes from what was originally built) and lateral buckling of the exterior beams during transport and erection (to explain buckling, picture squishing the two ends of a yardstick together; if you can picture how the ruler bows outward to one of the two skinny sides, that is buckling). The precasters provided a removable steel frame to support the beam during transport and installation.

The design team decided that the exterior beams should carry no live load from traffic. This was accomplished by adding steel brackets connecting the fascia beams to the adjacent steel beam and putting slotted holes in the connection between the interior and exterior beams, so the interior beams could deflect while the exterior beams would not receive any transferred load.

The construction worked as planned. The fascia beams look like the originals and after considering beam performance under load and making adjustments it proved to be a unique structural solution to aesthetics and environmental sensitivity.

                                                    -Tony Centore

Did you notice common lingo being used in both Brian and Tony's examples? Bridges bend under loads. Although sometimes engineers use complicated words, most words describe one of these:

- the loads that affect a structure,
- what happens to the structure when these loads are put on it,
- what the structure is made of and how strong it is,
- things that happen to the materials over time, and
- things that happen because of environmental reasons such as weather.

To dispel the illusion that all structural engineers work on bridges here is some "tech talk" from someone who does something very different.

In the Shop: John Looney

John Looney is the owner & president of JML Engineering and a Structural Specialist for the Federal Emergency Management Agency (FEMA) Massachusetts Task Force 1. John not only designs structures, but when disaster strikes and the governor of the state declares a State of Emergency, John flies out to keep the public safe and save people during emergencies.

Among other things, John had the unique honor of designing one of the craziest structures I've

ever seen: a giant ice cream sundae building
and a replica of the Massachusetts Capitol, both
completely coated with Jelly Belly® jellybeans
inside a furniture store.

*A Boston-area retailer that is noted for in-store
themed displays approached us to provide two
uniquely designed structures for their newest
store. The theme was a whimsical take on Boston
known as "Beantown." The structures are installed
on the second floor of a three-story building.*

*The first structure is an oversized banana split ice
cream sundae. The interior is a working ice cream
store (If you look very closely at the picture,
you can see it under the melting ice cream.) The
structure is thirty-eight feet high by fifty-four feet
wide by twenty feet deep. There are three scoops
and two fifty-four foot long bananas. One side of
this "sundae structure" is wide open for the ice*

cream serving counter. To make this work, the banana over the opening disguises to an oversized steel truss.

The other structure is a creative interpretation of the Massachusetts State House. The structure is three levels high with interior and exterior domes. The second level framing is designed to support and stabilize the open layout of the first level. There is a functioning candy store at the first level.

Decorative portions of the structures are constructed with one-inch square tube bent to form the basic shapes and covered with hardware cloth (picture a material similar to wire mesh or chicken wire, that has some strength but can easily be bent to make whatever shape is desired). Spray foam was then applied over the framework and carved to the final shape. The surfaces were covered with Jelly Belly® jellybeans coated with UV-resistant epoxy resin and multiple coats of flame proofing varnish. The inside of the structure has sprayed-on fireproofing. The architect's drawings indicated the location of each flavor, which then served as a color palette. In some locations multiple flavors were blended to achieve a specific color, such as when vanilla ice cream is a different color than whipped cream.

The final structures, along with some smaller displays, have over 60,000 pounds of jellybeans on them totaling approximately 25 Million jellybeans.

-John Looney

How fun would that be?! Could you imagine
designing something that you just cannot wait to
see in real life?

John would likely call this work an example
of "architectural engineering." Architectural
engineering, as the name suggests, is structural
engineering that is performed not to solve a public
problem, but to help architects achieve their
creative visions.

Whether the projects involve public infrastructure,
like bridges, or an architectural creation, the lingo
is much the same. Any structure that sits on the
earth needs geotechnical engineers designing
systems to keep it in place, and structural
engineers designing parts to withstand all other
forces and elements.

Designing Things to Move Along Nicely: Transportation and Traffic Engineers

Be it by foot, bike, horse, car, train, subway, boat, or plane, people like to get around. If we let nature have her way, this wouldn't always be so easy. Have you ever tried to run fast in deep woods? It is difficult to get by all the trees, let alone those nasty bramble patches that come up all too often. Sometimes we get a perfect stretch of open area in the perfect spot, but most often the easiest way to get around are on roads, which someone has to build[4].

Transportation and traffic sound similar, but in civil engineering, they have opposite meanings. While a transportation engineer wants to design smooth and free-flowing travel systems, the traffic engineer creates restraints on those systems to make them safer. While a transportation engineer would develop a set of travel ways, the traffic engineer would put in traffic lights in intersections to prevent smashups. Fortunately, these two groups of engineers are used to teaming up.

Travel ways are anything from footpaths, streets, highways, and runways, and the design depends on what type of travel the way supports.

---

4   Once we figure out teleportation, the future of transportation may change radically. What do you think?

Do you like playing in the sand at a beach? In certain ways, designing a travel way is really like a bigger version of playing in the sand. You take earth from around you and scoop it and form it into what you need. The big difference is that we don't want what we build to wash away (well, I guess we don't really want things we build on a beach to wash away either, but we're used to it).

To keep travel ways and roads from falling apart, engineers think about the materials and where rain might cause problems. Once you know the road is not going to break apart, then you think about the experience of those using your road. Are the turns too sharp, making the drivers feel like they will go flying off to the side? Is there a long line of vision to see what is coming at you? Are we aiming drivers at the sun for any long stretches? Is the road going somewhere that animals run across all the time?

Another major part of creating a new road is finding the place to put it. All property is pretty much owned by someone. Even if you work for the government, you can't start building wherever you want. You need to work out agreements with landowners. Also, roads can be devastating to natural resources and habitats. You need to know what you may wreck before you make anything, and you must study and create a way of preserving habitats. Anywhere you go, laws have been laid out and procedures in place to make sure people do not get their land unfairly taken, and that the environment gets fair consideration when creating a travel way.

So when you think of being a transportation engineer, think of yourself as part sculptor, part lawyer and part environmentalist.

In the Shop: Tom Taylor

Thomas T. Taylor is a civil engineer with Transystems. Tom specializes in railroad design, but very often designs highways and control systems for intersections as well. Tom recently moved from Boston to Cleveland.

An example that exemplifies a civil engineer's duties on a project would be the creation of a railroad spur. I was given the task of designing a new three-mile long railroad track to a quarry in Vermont (In railroad talk, there are mainline tracks and spurs. A mainline track just keeps going really long distances. Spurs are tracks that branch off the mainline to bring the train to a nearby destination. There's lots of other terms, too, but this will do for now.)

First I had to consider the requirements for railroad design. I had to remember that freight trains cannot travel up steep slopes and they must have long sweeping curves to stay on the track. With this in mind I had to look at the elevation of the quarry on one end, the elevation of the existing mainline track as it passed through the area at the other end, and the topography (shape) of the land in between.

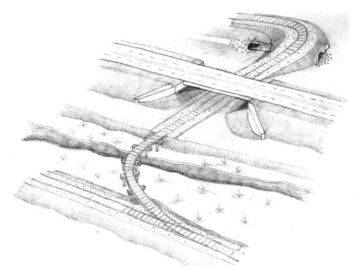

In this situation the quarry was located substantially higher than the track I needed to connect to, and there was a 90 foot tall ridge in between. I needed to find a path for the train that could go through the ridge without having steep slopes. This required that I cut a trough (in this case a trough is a long cut in the earth that does not have very steep sides) that was up to 20 feet deep through the ridge, and fill an embankment that was up to 40 feet tall to provide a ramp down to the existing track 3 miles away. Creating cuts of that depth and embankments of that height requires moving a tremendous volume of earth, which costs a lot of money.

An important way to keep costs down on projects like this is to try and balance the amount of earth that is cut in one location with the amount of fill that is needed in another. This way the builder doesn't need to pay as much to dispose of excess earth he just dug up from the cut and also doesn't need to pay as much for earth to be brought to the site to fill in the ramp area.

The next step in finding a path for the new railroad track was to look at the existing features that needed to be crossed or avoided. There were three different roadways that needed to be crossed, existing houses that needed to be avoided and wetlands that we didn't want to disturb too much. We needed to decide if we were going to cross the roadways with railroad crossings with flashers and gates, or if we were going to design bridges, so that the roadway traffic wouldn't have to stop for the slow train. We decided that bridges were the safest way to cross and had the least affect on local traffic. When comparing the different paths, we had to include the cost of building bridges which is primarily based on the height of the new bridge and the difference in the cuts and fills for the track to go over the bridge.

In order to make sure that the new track wouldn't be too close to existing houses and wetlands, we needed to take a look at how wide the path of the track was going to be. The taller or deeper an embankment or cut is, the wider the path for the track is going to be. With our embankment height *of 40 feet, the footprint (the outside edges of our work) was over 100 feet wide, fifty feet on either side of the track. In addition, we needed to make sure that the path for the new track was at least 50 feet away from any object that we wanted to avoid.*

So now, by following the requirements for railroad design it:

- *had long curves,*
- *had no steep slopes,*
- *crossed the existing roadways at a height that allowed roadway traffic to pass under the bridges,*
- *wasn't too tall,*
- *wasn't too expensive, and*
- *avoided existing houses and wetlands.*

By meeting this criteria, we could find the path of the new train track.

-Tom Taylor

This is a great example of the work of a transportation engineer and the design process all engineers use. To create the needed travel way, in this case a railroad spur, Tom drew up plans of how to reshape the earth and add structures to make this happen. He starts off by laying out on drawings exactly where everything presently is located and figures out in 3D how to best create his railroad in a way that only helps the neighborhood around the spur be better. He concerns himself with costs, with environmental impacts, and with effects on local roadway traffic. Tom worked in a team (which included my wife, Larisa) that:

- gathered all the necessary information (Step 1 of the engineering design process on page 15),
- brainstormed ways to get trains from the main track to their destination,
- figured out the best ideas and discussed them,
- drew up a final design, and
- put out the necessary documents for contractors to create this railroad spur.

While Tom's expertise is in the design of the railroad spur itself, the work of others is necessary to build this track. Geotechs will secure the earth, structurals will design bridges and walls to hold up the tracks, environmental engineers will take care of the permitting, and many others will have a part to play as well. In this case, many civil engineers together make a great team.

Designing Places People Like: Site Civil Engineers

Site civil engineers have a lot in common with transportation engineers, but instead of reshaping of the earth for a transportation project, site civil engineers develop a plan for real estate, be it a single building, a neighborhood, a recreation area, an industrial area, or another of the million types of developments. This work includes laying out the various components and getting the permission to build. Site civil engineers can work for communities or private entities to turn existing spaces into new places with a specific purpose, and that satisfy not only investors but everyone else with a say in the local community.

This "site" that is being designed needs to meet many requirements, which vary from community to community. Some rules are national, and some rules are local. In recent days, it has become more important to be environmentally conscious.

In the example on the next page, the site that is being engineered is a public school. As is typical in public building, architects take the lead and oversee the various engineers who each contribute their special knowledge to create an all-encompassing plan. As you can imagine, the design of a school is something that requires extra care:

- it has to be very safe,
- it has to be conducive to learning,
- it has to be accessible to everyone,
- it has to be adaptable, (every year the number of students changes, and so do the needs of a classroom! For example, 20 years ago, nobody thought schools would need a computer network.),
- it has to be durable, (schools take a lot of beating, be it by students, classroom activities or just natural occurrences like bad weather, and you will not always have budget to deal with maintenance later), and
- it has to be a beautiful place that students want to visit every day.

And the list could go on. A school is a huge investment for a community, and one that people care about deeply.

In the Shop: Cari Powers

Cari Powers is a site/civil engineer who is experienced in designing schools. Cari grew up in Maine and got her Bachelor of Science (BS) in Engineering from University of Maine in Orono. In 2010, she completed her master's degree at Worcester Polytechnic Institute (WPI) and became a Leadership in Energy and Environmental Design (LEED) Accredited Professional. She is a Professional Engineer licensed in the State of Rhode Island.

My company performed the site design for a proposed high school in Massachusetts. This high school was to be the first in the Model School Program in Massachusetts and is under review to be Collaborative for High Performance Schools (CHPS) certified. As the site engineers, we were subconsultants to an architecture firm which were the lead consultants on the project, coordinating all the disciplines of engineering. As the civil engineer on the project I was responsible for the site layout, hydrology, and hydraulic design for the storm water runoff, grading, and sewer design. In addition my company had two subconsultants working for us to provide the landscape and irrigation designs for the school.

One of the most important pieces of putting together the contract documents was advance and ongoing coordination with the project team and the town officials. Through coordination with the town, the school department, and the architect, we determined how many parking spaces were required and designed a parent drop-off and bus loop separate from one another to reduce traffic congestion during the peak times. Also, as part of the layout of the school site plan we designed locations for an athletic field in front of the school, tennis courts, a track, another athletic field and bleachers.

In addition to the basic site elements, we included locations for mechanical equipment like chillers (for the air conditioning), generators and transformers (for the school's electricity), and coordinated these elements with the mechanical engineers and town utility companies. Because there are certain restrictions on how close the mechanical units could be to the building and how much noise these systems generate, these were items that needed coordination near the beginning of the design. If we had wetlands or water bodies associated with the project, we would have had to submit paperwork to the local conservation commission or the State regulatory agency.

One major component of designing this high school was to grade the site in accordance to the American  Disability Act Guidelines (ADA). The change in elevation from one end of the site to the other was approximately 30 feet; so multiple ADA ramps were necessary, and ADA access was included on every pedestrian route. The number of ADA parking spaces and locations were also designed in accordance to the ADA guidelines.

The drainage design for the site consisted of designing the closed drainage system (a closed drainage system, basically, is one where people can't see the water, so really it means a bunch of pipes, so the design consisted of a drawing of the pipes, the size of each, and the amount each should slope), catch basin inlet capacities (a catch basin is those sewer grates you see along the sides of roads, plus the big box that is under that grate to catch all the water before it finds its way into the pipes), and manhole locations (manholes have solid covers on them and when you open the cover, there is a vertical pipe that leads you into the drainage pipe, often having ladder rungs on the sides, allowing maintenance workers to crawl into the pipes).

The hydrology component (my specialty) of the drainage design included three underground detention systems to prevent large amounts of gushing rainwater or melted snow from running off the property (flowing water like this can be the cause of major disasters, such as flooding roadways). The sewer design for the school consisted of the design of the pipes from the school to the street. Because the cafeteria has commercial grade kitchen equipment and serves the student population, a grease trap also had to be installed.

The project is now fully designed and construction is beginning. Throughout the construction process we will provide on call

services when shop drawings and requests for information (RFI's) come in from the contractor. If modifications to our plans are required during the construction phase we will provide sketches. Another important and valuable part of the construction phase is site visits, so the engineer can review and observe the work as it is being completed, but also so the engineer can truly see what was once on paper come to life.
-Cari Powers

Like all engineering fields, there are an amazing variety of different sectors within the civil engineering world. Cari works in the private sector for an engineering firm. There are many civil engineers who work directly for government agencies. Whether a small town or a big city, there is a infrastructure that must be kept running. Sewer systems need to function with each and every flush, roads must be drivable, and faucets must supply water that is good. Much of this work first falls into the hands of the government. On both the small and large scale, from towns to the federal government and the military, engineers are needed to make sure all communities get the services they need.

Once in a while, there is an engineer that does not work for a consultant, a client, or a contractor. Lisa Freed is such an engineer. Lisa works for a law firm. There are close ties between the law profession and civil engineering because any infrastructure project needs to follow books of legal codes.

In the Shop: Lisa Freed

If you are familiar with "Sim City" or the Future City Competition, you may notice how Lisa Freed's real work resembles Sim City. She works on many different zones within a community, and must conform with community regulations and requirements. Lisa Freed is the pioneer of the Future City Competition for New England and she is a LEED certified civil engineer with a Masters degree in Landscape Architecture from Harvard.

The client approached his legal counsel having recently purchased land in a small suburban New England town. He desired to develop the 30-acre site into townhouse condominiums with some garden-style condos. The lot contained an abandoned 7-acre parking lot, a small stream, wetlands, and neglected baseball field. So, the town was certainly interested in ridding itself of the eyesore, but the process to get there would be somewhat complex.

The first step was to review the zoning of the lot. Because it was a single lot in an industrial zone, multiple dwelling units on one lot were not allowed. To go forward, the lot would need to be rezoned to allow for the condo-style development.

The attorney drafted a new residential zoning
district and the engineers prepared a draft
site plan to present to the town selectman (an
executive board of 3-5 people) and planning
board. With their support, the next step was to
present the zoning change to a town meeting.
In many traditional New England towns, town
meetings approve such changes, requiring town
residents to vote for approval.

With some heavy marketing, and strong appeal
from local constituents, the client managed to get
the zoning change approved. Working in his favor
was a strong appeal from the local youth baseball
group, to whom the developer offered to restore
the field and donate it to the town for playing
space.

With the zoning in place, the engineers began
the formal design process. First, the site plan
needed to be reviewed by the planning board
and a special permit issued. The planning board
questioned, revised, and offered comments for
months until a plan with appropriate density,
mix of units, parking, drainage, landscape
and appealing amenities was presented. The
planning board also requested many "off site"
improvements, including construction of sidewalks
to connect pedestrians to the nearby rail trail,
and an upgrade to the water line and sewer pump
station which would be used by the development.

The project also promised to maintain a certain
number of the townhouse units as affordable.

The planning board, housing partnership, and the state government reviewed the plan for the affordable units to be sure they targeted the appropriate income levels and would offer fair opportunity for purchase.

All aspects of the project were presented to the selectman, who entered a development agreement to commit the developer to the stated number of units presented, the affordable unit marketing, the donation of the ball field, and municipal infrastructure upgrades, among other things.

Of course, the site also contained wetlands, necessitating an order of conditions from the Conservation Commission. The Commission held many meetings to negotiate an appropriate plan that improved the wetland areas, added trail walks and restored much of the natural habitat. The site was also within the town's designated flood plain district, so the plan was presented to the zoning Board of Appeals with a request for a special permit to allow development within the flood plain. The plan allowed for compensation of any work disturbing the flood plain, and removed much of the impervious (not penetrable) material currently on site, and therefore was seen as beneficial by the zoning Board.

Finally, to complicate matters further, the site was next to an area in which there had been a former release of hazardous materials. Residents raised concerns that a plume of the hazardous waste *could conceivably spread through the aquifer in the area, contaminate this site, and threaten the use of the restored baseball field. A geotechnical engineering study ensued and proof offered that the site remained clean and that the adjoining site had continuing monitoring to insure safety.*

After months and months of meetings, the project finally had all of the permits and permissions, and construction could now begin.

-Lisa Freed

If you thought that civil engineering was all math and science, I hope you see that the work can be very different and full of people after reading about Lisa's work. Civil engineers like Lisa discuss marketing, fight legal battles, attend and lead public discussions, and maintain permits. But, that work is a major part of the design process: without public approval and understanding, some projects simply do not happen.

The issues that arise in a site civil project are common to many civil engineering projects including the design of sports facilities.

In the Shop: Sarah Campbell

Sara Campbell is a site civil engineer in Western Massachusetts and writes of the internal debates engineers have with themselves as they design.

Sara runs her own engineering firm and is at present hard at work as a resident engineer for a project at the University of Massachusetts in Amherst. She has a Masters in Civil Engineering specializing in hydrology, and she has an MBA.

Here in New England there aren't many "wide open spaces" because the landscape is full of wandering rivers and mountains, large or small. When it is time to build, we have to work with this topographic landscape, or change it to suit the project.

Sometimes buildings can be set into a hillside, or large parking lots can have many levels, but this isn't true for athletic fields. How would you go about planning for construction of sports facilities?

Usually, the standards for the size and shape and slope of fields are set by governing organizations, like the NFL or International Olympic Committee. We know that football fields are measured precisely to be 100 yards long. But what would a topographic map of a football field look like? Would it be fair if one end was several feet higher than the other? One team would be running uphill on offense and the other team would be running downhill. What if it were built in a valley and the 50-yard line was lower than the end zones? On a rainy day there would be a big puddle standing in the middle of the field. For these reasons site engineers have to pay close attention to the grading plan for athletic fields.

Here are some of the questions that are asked when someone wants to build athletic fields:

- *Who owns the land? The field might be at a school or a town park, or it might be a piece of property that is owned by someone else for forest or farmland and will be bought to build a field. Often the first step is to measure the land with a Boundary Survey to see how much land is available.*

- *How steep is the land? If the field has to be almost flat, and the site is on a mountain, it may be too expensive to put all of that soil in dump trucks and haul it away. Or it might be very hard rock, and require dynamite to break it up, which is even more expensive. The topographic survey will give the engineer a way to start calculating how much the ground will change and how much that will cost.*

- *Which way is north, south, east, or west? You wouldn't want to play baseball or softball on a field where the batter is always trying to see the pitches with the sun in his or her eyes. Most organized sports take place in the late afternoon, so the direction of the sunset is important to consider.*

* *What way does the water drain when it rains? Wet fields are dangerous fields. Slipping can cause serious injuries to athletes. If water from the ground above the field flows down every time it rains and floods the field, it might stay wet for days afterward. If the land is flat because it is swampy, there will be lots of mosquitoes near the fields. Land that is swampy, and sometimes land that doesn't look wet during part of the year, may be protected by the state and the town as wetlands. It may take a long and difficult process to get approval to build on the land which is near a wetland, even if the wetland itself is not*

disturbed. Usually a series of underground drainage pipes are needed to dry out the moist ground and direct the runoff away. Rectangular fields for football and soccer are usually designed with a crown that directs runoff off the center of the fields and with a very gentle slope from end to end, or no slope at all, or slightly higher in the middle. The bigger the budget for the project is, the more you can change the topography to make the field perfect. Most of the time the owner of the project wants to keep the cost low.

- What type of dirt is under there anyway? We already thought about how difficult it would be to blast a rocky hillside for a playing field. It is a balancing act to make sure the soil under the field is sandy enough to take away the runoff, but not too dry so the grass won't grow. Think about how water disappears when poured in a hole at the beach. Sand doesn't hold water. But don't try to grow a green lawn at the beach without lots of topsoil. Remember, school sports seasons start when the snow is barely gone in cold climates, and are finished when school gets out in June, so the time the fields will be used is important to keep in mind during the design. The ability to grow healthy hearty grass when little feet are constantly running on a field can be difficult. How do you feel about artificial turf surfaces? Running tracks often have a rubberized surface, but all of these

things cost money. You can research various
materials and their costs fairly easily on the
internet.

- Wait, why did we want this field anyway?
One of the most important things an
engineer can do is to listen to the client.
A grammar school doesn't need fields that
are of Olympic caliber. Someone who has
access to a nearby gravel pit might lower
the construction cost of bringing in drainage
materials substantially. If a specific mowing
machine will be used, that might affect how
steep the slopes will be or how wide the
spaces between fences or bleachers might
be. Sometimes engineers like to think of
themselves as experts in EVERYTHING they
do, but they should not forget to listen to
people who might not be engineers but who
have great ideas.

- Where in the world are the spectators
going? The players don't drop from
spaceships to play on our athletic fields.
They might come in a bus and that requires
a big parking space and room to turn
around. Even if the team arrives in a bus,
their fans will likely drive to the field to
watch. Usually cars can't park on the side
of the road. Safe parking will have to be
located around the field. And don't forget
about those foul balls that can go through
windshields! Will there be a concession
stand? Will it have running water? How
about restrooms? Is there a sewer line

available or will they bring in portable facilities as needed? Sometimes it seems like every question leads to more questions.

Engineering is all about making decisions and weighing options that consider a wide variety of possibilities, including how much each decision will affect the cost of the project. It is also very important to understand the end user. When a project is complete, it is very rewarding to see people enjoying something that started as an idea on paper. In little ways like this, engineers know they can change the world around them.

The more happy users or owners you have, the better your reputation will be.

-Sarah Campbell

The last sentence says a lot. The goal of anyone developing a site, or performing the design of any infrastructure-related project, should always have the end user in mind, and make every effort to assure that once the project is finished, the user will be satisfied with what you have been instrumental in creating.

.

Designing with Community Needs in Mind: Government Engineers

The word "civil" means community, and whether it is used to mean a neighborhood or a country, it is often the communities themselves that put together civil engineering projects. At any level of government, a certain number of engineers have to be on hand to react quickly to a need and make sure it is addressed, whether they initiate a project to be done by an engineering firm or they provide the design themselves. It is the duty of these government engineers to have their eyes open to spot the issues to address and to assure that, in the end, the solution proposed is going to work.

David Manugian is a municipal engineer for a town in Massachusetts. Some issues municipal engineers handle themselves, and for other issues, they hire consultants to recommend solutions.

In the Shop: David Manugian

David is the Town Engineer for Oxford, Massachusetts. He is also the newsletter editor for the Boston Society of Civil Engineers.

*I am a municipal engineer. I help design and
oversee the infrastructure in a community that
helps improve the quality of the residents' lives.
Often this infrastructure is not noticed unless
there is a problem. It includes roads, bridges,
sewer systems, water systems, flood control,
dams, and drainage systems. Some of the
projects I have worked on include reconstructing
old roads where the existing pavement is
falling apart; redesigning culverts to better
accommodate stream flows; investigating existing
dams for their potential to generate hydroelectric
power; helping the local Little League develop
lighting for one of their ball fields; and improving
the municipalities' drainage system in areas
where there is frequent flooding.*

*Municipal engineers represent their community
when working with developers, contractors, other
communities, and state agencies on infrastructure
projects. Each of these parties may have an
interest in the proposed infrastructure project. On
a typical project the engineer develops conceptual
designs; prepares design plans, technical
specifications, and construction estimates;
oversees construction bidding; and reviews the
progress of work during construction.*

*I also review development projects proposed for
the community to ensure that they meet federal,
state, and municipal development regulations
pertaining to infrastructure. These reviews
often deal with making sure that stormwater
from the property being developed does not*

adversely impact neighboring properties or municipal roadways. The developer's engineers create models to simulate stormwater flow for a variety of storm events. They must show that stormwater peak flows do not exceed those prior to development or increase flooding to adjacent properties. They must also show that stormwater quality is maintained or improved so as not to pollute downstream water bodies. I then review their models for accuracy.

The jobs of a municipal engineer can vary widely. A municipal engineer in a small town may work on his or her own and get a little involved in many different types of projects, whereas an engineer working for a large city may be part of a large staff and become very experienced in one or two types of projects or activities. Of all the things I do, one of the most enjoyable parts of my job is using my education and experience to help residents solve problems so that the infrastructure around them runs efficiently and effectively.

-Dave Manugian

A second type of government engineer is the military engineer. Our military is also very involved with what we call civil engineering projects. While many people hear the word "military" and automatically tie the word to combat, this is not typically the case. Of course, the goal of the military is the national defense, but the work of engineers in the military is far broader than preparing fortifications for combat. After an area has experienced combat or any natural disaster, military engineers will often undertake the task of rebuilding damaged infrastructure. The Army Corps of Engineers is the largest resource of military engineers in the country, and is dedicated to protecting the country in ways far different than the military. They protect and maintain our coasts and waterways, clean environmental messes, and rush to the rescue in the event of disasters all around the world. They also design bridges and roads for the purpose of making evacuation or access by emergency vehicles easier in the event of an emergency. Chan Rogers, one of the most distinguished members of the American Society of Civil Engineers offers this brief history of military engineering and tells about his experience as an engineer in the Reserves.

In the Shop: Cranston "Chan" Rogers

Chan Rogers is a retired structural engineer, but is still active in many projects, particularly at the planning stage. He is a former President of the American Society of Civil Engineers. During World War II, Chan was among the troops that liberated the concentration camps. He has been a leader in design, working on both Central Artery projects through downtown Boston and countless other projects as well. He also led a team of engineers during rescue efforts after Hurricane Katrina in Louisiana, and has long given service to this country as an Army Reserve Platoon Leader.

The term "Military Engineering" first emerged in the late 18th century as the colonists prepared for a revolution to gain our independence. It was used in the context of describing the activities involved in the construction of fortifications, specifically at Breed's Hill (AKA "Bunker Hill"). Military Engineering then became the dominant form of engineering taught in the first colleges established at Rensselaer and West Point (The US Military Academy) during the early 19th Century. However, as our young country moved west, canal construction dominated to facilitate our westward movement by linking Lake Erie, Lake Ontario, the Mohawk River, and then the Hudson River to New York City. It was during this period that the term "civil engineering" was applied to all works of man involving civil infrastructure pursuits (non-military as opposed to his military endeavors). It should also be noted that the term "engineering" when used by the military, generally refers to construction of facilities as opposed to planning and design of facilities. In fact, today, the US Army has an extensive array of sophisticated military units devoted to the construction of specific types of support of the military as it operates in undeveloped countries and they are all titled "Engineering" or "Construction" units to build roads, bridges, petroleum pipelines, establish water points (for delivery of drinking water), and to construct semi-permanent buildings. Currently, the US Army has, by far, the greatest array of units and the greatest capacity of any army in the world for construction of support facilities. However, now in the 21st century, it appears we are able to contract private sector companies to perform such missions.

With this in mind, I would like to introduce myself, Cranston "Chan" Rogers. Having served in the army during World War II, I thereafter remained in  *the army reserve so as to be ready to serve my country if needed, and in due time, I commanded a US Army Reserve Combat Engineer Battalion during the timeframe 1965-73. In that capacity, my unit and I received several commendations for the outstanding accomplishments made while training my battalion by completing over 45 major projects that benefited many cities and towns, non-profit charities, and church groups in southeastern Massachusetts - three little league baseball fields with backstops, an under-privileged children's camp dining hall, lion's den at the New Bedford zoo, a ski slope and warming huts in North Attleboro are just some examples. In addition to being recognized as the*

most outstanding civic-action unit in the entire country, my unit was also cited by the Army Chief of Engineers for outstanding engineering work and by the First Army Commander for having the highest re-enlistment rate of any unit in that area. All men in the unit from the commander down to the last man were excited and pleased to be a part of this very practical training (hence the high re-enlistment rate) and furthermore all were very pleased to be able to work providing facilities for the young and less fortunate people to enjoy.
                                                    -Chan Rogers

Can you see why there was such a high re-enlistment rate? Chan wanted to keep his unit well trained in the event that they were needed for an emergency response. To keep his unit trained, he continually undertook great community service activities, and the great feeling you get in undertaking such work is something everyone should experience. To this day, even at his present age of 87 years young, Chan continues to dedicate himself to serving the public.

Designing to Keep the Water Away: Civil Engineers in the Water

Earth is really a pretty strange place. When you look down at it from a plane, it is a swirly mess of land and water, and although we make maps and globes all the time, water does not stay put. Water dries out, other water eats away at the land, and some changes its path. When building infrastructure, which we build to either simplify our life or protect the planet from us, you want water to stay put.

We build bridges over rivers all the time, and generally do a good job putting them in the right places for the short term, but Mother Nature might have a different plan for that river. We have two choices: either go with the flow and adapt, or try to persuade Nature. Either way, civil engineers head up the battle. Deep rooted in good civil engineering is a boatload  of respect for Mother Nature; she is extremely powerful and can rip apart a poorly planned or executed project.

Rivers are just one of the multitude of water formations. When you look at a globe, oceans jump right out, and as anyone who has spent time along a coastline knows, the crashing, ripping force of Mother Nature can unleash on beaches and other coastal land.

Listen to the news; it will not be long before you hear some awful story of coastal structures taking the full brunt of an ocean's impact. However, if it were not for civil engineers, you would hear those stories much more often. Engineers save lives.

We will hear from engineers who face challenges from oceans, but first, let's consider ponds and lakes. Ponds most often form naturally. Water can collect from brooks and streams into an open bowl-shaped area. Especially in places with a small area for flow, water from melting snow and rain can amass near material that water cannot pass through. A river can change its course, sealing and covering portions of its old streambed (we call that an oxbow).

There are hundreds of different ways a pond can form naturally. However, David "Doc" Westerling of Merrimack College writes of when humanity wants ponds in places that they do not naturally form.

Shop Talk: David Westerling

David "Doc" Westerling is a professor at Merrimack College. He is also the Region 1 Governor for ASCE and has been their Congressional Fellow. After Hurricane Katrina, Doc took off time from his regular work to be a supervisory forensic engineer in New Orleans.

Ponds are great! You can swim and fish, hunt for frogs, skip flat stones across the surface, all kinds of stuff. You also need them for freshwater to drink. On golf courses they provide water for keeping the greens green. Some of the ones I've helped to build are used for watering cows and horses, for ice skating in the winter, and for irrigating cranberries on Cape Cod.

To design a pond, you start by finding a good flat stream with a large drainage area. And then you have to mound up soil to build the dam. The soil has to be a clay soil or a fine silt that will not let water pass through it. A clean sand or gravel won't work for a dam (Think about a bucket of sand or gravel with a hole in the bottom – every drop you pour into that bucket is going to drain right out the hole. This is a bad thing when you are trying to hold back the water!)

Inside the mound is a pipe called a spillway so you can control the water level in the pond. And don't forget the emergency spillway that is carved into the land near the dam. This allows stormwater to go around the dam so it won't wash out. These storms may only occur once every one hundred years or so, so we call that a 100-year storm.

Finally you have to provide for the plants and animals that live near the stream and will now live in the pond. This includes wetland grasses and sedges, willows and red maple trees, and maybe even pond lilies where frogs can lay in the sun. Sunfish and Smallmouth Bass love the warm water along the shores of the pond. And if the pond is deep enough, Rainbow Trout will live in the cool waters down below.

I visit the ponds I've helped to design and build over the years. I go there to watch the plants and wildlife and it makes me feel good all over. There is nothing quite like a pond.

- David "Doc" Westerling

This is a great example of civil engineering working with Mother Nature to create something good for everybody. I would be remiss if I did not mention that some projects in history were less respectful of surrounding ecology. Some people think "dam" is a four-letter word because when you build a dam on a river or stream, you block water upstream and take away water downstream.

The projects that Doc is speaking about pay close attention to give and take. If the impact of a dam are not carefully studied and considered in the design, the effects on people and the whole environment upstream and downstream can be devastating. Life on land needs the right amount of water. Whole societies have disappeared because of a lack of water, and a large dam can put areas upstream totally under water. It is the job of civil engineers to consider the design and to be vigilant in addressing any impacts.

The most common news stories involving humans versus water involves either oceans or very large lakes. Humanity has been protecting shorelines and coastal communities from floods and tides for centuries. Every so often, water adds one to the win column, and people have to rebuild.

Shop Talk: Carlos Pena

Carlos Pena is a Vice President at CLE Engineering, a certified diver and an authority on the design of coastal structures. He is also a past president of the Boston Society of Civil Engineers.

Our firm designed emergency seawall repairs for a 25 foot high section of vegetated coastal bank along a popular island beach. The original concrete retaining wall structure along this section of beach had been designed as a training wall for a coastal railroad at the turn of the century. An

adjacent 100-foot section of similarly designed
seawall had collapsed earlier in the winter
following a winter storm event threatening a
major state roadway and public utilities.

The remaining 200-foot section of seawall had
been converted to public use and supported the
coastal bank behind town recreational facilities.
Initial inspections of the remaining seawall
determined the original training wall was failing
due to excessive seaward rotation, differential
settlement, major longitudinal and horizontal
cracks, lack of a proper steel reinforcement and
an undersized footing.

The first step in assessing the condition of the
seawall was to perform a topographic survey
to define the existing conditions and provide
design parameters for engineering evaluations
and repair designs. The geotechnical conditions
were determined by the performance of
standard penetration tests (SPT) to determine
the underlying sediment properties. The typical
sediment attributes defined by a SPT include
grain size, unit weight and internal angle of
friction. Performance of an infinite slope analysis
determined the existing coastal bank had slope
pitch exceeding 33 degrees and a calculated
Factor of Safety (FS) of between 1.0 and 1.12
well below the recommended FS of 1.5 for the site
conditions.

Additional repair design considerations include
100-year flood elevations, impacts from storm-

driven waves, future sea level rises and sediment transport rates along with potential beach erosion. A number of repair alternatives were evaluated including (1) replacement of the seawall, (2) bracing and (3) burial of the entire structure under an engineered slope.

The town evaluated the three repair options and along with public input, consideration of estimates for repair costs, project durations, and the potential disruption of the summer season, and selected the burial option. The coastal bank restoration project was completed before the beginning of the summer season. The engineered slope was constructed according to plans and specifications and planted with salt-tolerant beach grass to create a stable coastal structure, enhanced coastal habitat, and safe public access to the beach.

-Carlos Pena

Think back to the design cycle at the beginning of this book. I added a loop to the design cycle that makes mine different from others I have seen in school curriculum. This additional loop involves paying attention to what is built and figuring out when something is wrong. A key ingredient in this part of the cycle is inspection. Inspection is scheduling time to pay close attention to infrastructure elements, take inventory of components, and evaluate the condition and effectiveness of each. I personally love inspection and the climbing that can go with it.

Shop Talk: Charlie Roberts

Charlie Roberts of Childs Engineering loves diving and combines this with his work as he performs underwater inspections.

I am a waterfront structural engineer and I specialize in the design and inspection of structures that are built in the marine environment, where the land meets the ocean. Typical projects include ferry terminals, piers, marinas, and seawalls. One element of my work is underwater inspection. Nearly

all structures along the waterfront are partially submerged and therefore not all of the structure can be seen from the surface. The only way to inspection these structures is underwater. I am an engineer first, but I am also a certified commercial SCUBA diver, which gives me the skills to perform structural inspections underwater.

I recently completed a routine underwater inspection for the US Navy on a 3000-foot pier that is used to load the Navy's ships with supplies and ammunition. Before we mobilized to inspect the pier, we prepared a safety plan that listed all the emergency contacts, identified any risks we might encounter, and recommended ways in which we can minimize these risks to make the job site as safe as possible.

For Naval facilities we are required to dive under the US Army Corps of Engineers' regulations. As we were diving from the pier we chose to dive with surface supplied air, this method uses a compressor to send filtered air from the surface, down an air hose in the umbilical, to the divers helmet so they can breathe. The divers also have

a bail out tank on their backs that provides an additional source of air if they lose the air supply from the surface. We used a 5-person dive team consisting of a supervisor, who runs the diving operation, two divers, who conduct the underwater inspection, and two tenders, who make sure the divers have enough umbilical and it is not getting tangled. As the entire job took two weeks we rotated through each of the positions.

Each morning we set up the equipment and performed our safety checks to make sure it was all functioning properly. The dive supervisor then briefed the dive team so we would understand our objectives for the dive. The two divers were then dressed-in and pre-dive checks performed before climbing down the ladder and into the water.

Once in the water the divers begin the underwater inspection. This pier was comprised of 16-inch square, concrete piles that were spaced 4 to 6 feet apart. Each of the piles was carefully inspected by descending down the piles and feeling to see if there were any major defects, such as broken areas or large sections of the pile missing, which would typically occur during an impact with an object such as a ship. This level of visual inspection is referred to as a Level One inspection. As the visibility was less than 1 foot and all the piles were covered with thick marine growth most of the inspection was done by feel, rather than sight.

A more detailed, Level Two, inspection was conducted on 10% of the piles. This required removing a band of the marine growth at the top, middle, and bottom of the pile. Once the bare concrete pile was visible, a detailed inspection could be conducted. Typical defects found included abrasions, cracks, and corrosion spalls.

These defects and their locations were then communicated to the supervisor on the surface via the communication wires in the umbilical. The supervisor at the control station is able to continuously hear both divers which allows them to be monitored at all times and also provides a means of communication with each diver. The *supervisor also monitors the air quality and pressure being delivered to the divers.*

Once the section of the pier being completed was done, the divers returned to the ladder and climbed back up to the pier where the tenders helped remove all the dive equipment. After the dive, the dive supervisor debriefed the team and clarified any notes that had been hard to describe underwater.

Back at the office we compiled a set of drawings showing the type and location of the defects that we had found and made recommendations on how to repair the defects.

-Charlie Roberts

Charlie does not only inspect marine structures, he also designs them. Below, Charlie talks about a project aimed at protecting a shoreline from the raging water during storms:

I designed a revetment (A revetment is a sloping structure that, in this case, absorbs wave energy and prevents erosion) to protect a structure that was being damaged during storms. The revetment was intended to replace the existing slope that did not have adequate protection. The slope was covered in large rocks and boulders but they were not packed together closely which allowed the waves to wash out the material beneath the rocks and undermine the slope. This undermining was causing the structure at the top of the slope to be potentially unstable.

We were asked to provide a design that would prevent the slope from eroding any further, and therefore protect the structure at the top. We went out to the site to conduct a site survey. This involved using a survey level to determine the elevation at different parts of the structure so we could calculate the current slope. As we did not want to alter the existing slope we decided that we would rehabilitate the slope instead.

In order to design the slope correctly we needed to determine the correct size of stone that we would use to protect the slope. We calculated the forces that the waves could place on the slope by analyzing the distance the wind could travel uninterrupted, the depth of the seabed, and the slope of the seabed on the approach. These calculations allowed us to determine the size of rock needed for the different layers of the revetment that will be constructed, specifically the armor layer and the filter layer.

Each layer has a specific purpose; the armor layer has large rocks that are sized so they will not move significantly in a large storm. These large rocks dissipate the initial force of the wave energy due to their irregular shape and spacing. However the spacing between the rocks in the armor layer still allows the wave to partially pass through. The filter layer is therefore constructed of smaller and tighter packed rocks that further dissipate the wave energy and help protect the slope from being eroded underneath. In this design the slope that we were protecting was composed of fine sand and therefore we added a filter fabric to help further minimize the erosion of the slope.

Our design involved excavating a trench at low tide and placing the largest stones at the base of the slope to form the toe. The toe of the slope is very important because it locks the rest of the slope in place. Rocks that were not large enough for the toe would then be removed and the filter fabric placed. Smaller rocks and boulders would then be placed on top of the filter fabric to create the filter layer. On top of the filter layer large stones and boulders, slightly smaller than those used in the toe, would then be placed to create the armor layer.

Once the revetment had been designed, we produced a plan and cross section of how the slope should appear. These plans were initially used to show the federal, state and local permitting and regulatory agencies what we were planning on doing, and to allow any neighbors to voice their concerns at a public meeting. Once we had all the relevant approvals, we completed the construction documents by adding additional construction notes to the drawings, producing a set of specifications to outline the type of materials to be used and how to use them, and compiled a cost estimate.

After the construction documents had been reviewed by our client, we sent the documents to various contractors that had expressed interest in bidding on the job. Once all the bids had come back from the contractors, we selected one with our client.

During the construction process we made regular site visits to make sure that the work was being done in accordance to our plans and to answer any questions or address problems the contractor had. The project took several weeks to complete and is presently holding strong.

-Charlie Roberts

Take a moment to think about the affect that the work of engineers like Charlie and Carlos can have on the lives of people living near the coast. Without these seawalls or revetments, communities could get swallowed up by crashing waves and flooding tides.

They perform their work daily without any fanfare and without the media extolling the virtue of their efforts, but their work saves lives—plain and simple. And there is a certain pride they take in doing their work knowing that they are doing something important. But this pride also includes the civil engineers that not only battle against water, but also those involved with other aspects of civil engineering such as:

- treating waste to prevent disease,
- providing clean drinking water,

- assuring that the roads, bridges and tunnels are safe,
- making sure that the earth will hold beneath a structure, or
- doing other tasks in design and maintenance of our infrastructure.

Many civil engineers can and do take pride in making life better for people and helping sustain our planet and all the life on it.

Designing to Keep it Clean: Environmental, Water, and Wastewater Engineers

You cannot say enough about the importance of keeping our planet clean. Not a day goes by without some mention of pollution, the damage we have done to our environment, and many "green" initiatives. This is not new news in the civil engineering world. Clean water and treatment of waste are critical to both people and other parts of nature's survival.

Clean water has been an issue for thousands of years, and ancient Egyptian and Sanskrit writings mention desalinization as far back as 2000 BC. Wastewater was recognized as an issue in ancient Rome, which had open sewers. The ideas for meeting the need for clean water took hold in the 1600's amidst one of the worst periods of plague in history. In the 1800's, sewer-system design took off and over the next two hundred years, led to the wastewater treatment plants we see today. The effect of their improvements on the quality of life all over the world is remarkable.

Shop Talk: Dan Saulnier

Dan Saulnier is a proud member of an organization called Engineers Without Borders (EWB) that lead projects to improve the quality of life for people all over the world. Dan is one of the leaders of the Boston-area chapters and describes a project he was involved with through EWB.

With a team from EWB, I helped a small village in the mountains of Honduras in Central America build a system of pipes and tanks to bring clean drinking water to their homes. Before the project, they had to hike down to a polluted river and carry buckets of dirty water

back uphill to their homes. They were often sick and malnourished because of the water, and young children would often die. Now they open faucets in their front yards and get cool, clean spring water. They are healthier and happier, and have extra water for growing vegetables.

Here in the United States, engineers design complicated water treatment plants to make sure the water from the tap is safe to drink. These treatment plants are full of equipment and special chemicals that pull impurities out of the water, and are run by people trained to ensure the water is always clean and pure. In the village of Los Planes, Honduras, they have no money for fancy equipment or chemicals, and there's no electricity to run pumps and other systems we have here. They need a water system that can run by itself, and that's where EWB got involved.

I traveled down to Honduras with a team of five engineering students from Northeastern University. We brought with us water-testing supplies, surveying equipment, and a GPS tracking device. We ran tests on the stream water they were drinking, looking especially at bacteriological contamination. The stream was in an area that had been stripped of its natural vegetation and replaced with farmland, logging areas and animal pastures; the stream water was polluted.

No maps had ever been made of Los Planes, so we asked a local man to sketch one for us, and then we used our GPS equipment to fine-tune it. With the villagers' help, we found a natural spring high up on a mountain about two miles away from the village. We ran the same tests on this water, as well as taking flow measurements to see how much water the spring was producing. The spring was surrounded by Honduras's natural ecosystem, and the water was clean. We used our surveying equipment to make a detailed map of the route between the spring and the village, and the elevation differences along the way. This would become a critical piece of information when designing the water system.

We then designed a system to capture the spring water and run it through pipes down the mountain, through a valley, across two ravines, and up to a storage tank on a hill above the village. We then designed a system of smaller pipes and valves to bring the water from the storage tank to each family's house in the village. The whole system was powered by the force of gravity. The weight of water coming into the pipeline at the spring pushes down on the water at the low points in the valley. The water at the low points can't escape the pipeline, so it can

only go one direction when pushed from the spring: uphill to the village of Los Planes. This design resulted in extremely high water pressure in the pipes at the low points in the valley, so we had to find extra-strength pipes that could handle this pressure (about  four times the pressure in your home). The team had to complete a series of hydraulic calculations to make sure this system would work.

The spring produces a small amount of water, but produces that small amount 24 hours per day, 7 days per week. The villagers need a lot of water, but only at certain times of day when doing laundry, cooking, etc. That's where the water storage tank comes in. When people in the village aren't using water (like in the middle of the night), the storage tank has more water coming in than going out, and so it fills up. In the morning, when everyone gets up and begins to wash and make breakfast, the demand for water is greater than

the supply from the spring, and the difference is made up by the storage tank, which starts to empty. One of our tasks as engineers was to make sure the tank was big enough to allow this cycle of filling and emptying to sustain the villagers' water use.

Crossing the two ravines (each ravine was about 100 feet across and three or four stories deep)

turned out to be a big problem. But engineering is about solving problems, and we ended up building miniature suspension bridges *out of steel pipe and steel cables, and we hung the pipeline from the bottom of these bridges.*

Construction of the project was a team effort between the group of us from EWB and the people living in the village. We contributed technical equipment and engineering knowledge, and they contributed local know-how and a seemingly endless supply of hard work. The entire project, including two miles of trench for the pipeline, was constructed by hand, using picks and shovels and muscles.

We spent our evenings doing engineering calculations, planning construction activities, and figuring out solutions to new problems that kept cropping up. We spent our days working from sunrise to sunset, hiking up mountains in 95°F heat, climbing through barbed wire fences, hauling pipes, tools and surveying equipment around, and trying to learn Spanish. We would stop for a lunch of bean burritos and water, and would often be sitting on the side of a hill, looking at the rolling green mountains surrounding us, and chatting with each other and our new Honduran friends. We learned a lot about the way many people in the world lead their lives, from the challenges of poverty and lack of educational opportunity to the pleasures of living off the land and being surrounded by close family ties.

-Dan Saulnier

Bravo, Dan! Remember this is a volunteer effort he has undertaken, and he does more work than most people do on vacation.

Remember how important waste disposal can be in civil design? Most people think this means dumps and sewers, but waste disposal covers a gamut of topics from many different fields.

Shop Talk: Katherine Saltanovitz

Katie Saltanovitz is an environmental engineer at Brown & Caldwell specializing in landfills. She recently moved to Seattle and is already working with ASCE on a popsicle stick bridge competition for high school kids.

My team and I designed a vertical expansion of an existing solid waste landfill, which included

three new landfill cells with 1,300,000 cubic yards (845,000 tons) of waste disposal volume—enough for about 9 years of operation. By expanding the landfill vertically, we gained additional airspace without expanding the existing landfill footprint into the wetlands that border the site.

This design required us to use a wide range of engineering skills, including site design, drafting, geotechnical engineering, transportation engineering, hydraulics, construction management, environmental science, geology, public relations, and report writing. Because solid waste facilities are tightly controlled, we started by reviewing the state and local regulations to make sure our design met all these requirements.

Next, we evaluated existing conditions at the landfill site, including groundwater, surface water, soil, nearby wildlife habitat and residential areas, traffic flow, air quality, and other factors that could be affected by the construction of new cells. We summarized our findings in a report and also presented them at a public meeting to help residents understand the landfill development plan and have a chance to ask questions. Once the state determined that our proposed expansion met environmental protection requirements, we focused on the technical design.

Because the new cells would be constructed over existing waste, we evaluated the geotechnical static and seismic stability of the landfill to be sure that the new cells would have a stable foundation. We designed the new cells with a double composite liner system, which uses layered geosynthetic materials to create a leak-proof seal that prevents leachate from escaping the landfill. Our design also included calculations of the required interface friction angles, flow capacity of the drainage materials, predictions of leachate generation, and head *losses in the leachate pumping system. We designed submersible pumps to move leachate from collection pipes inside the landfill cell to a force main outside the cell, and from there to the town's wastewater treatment plant.*

Because landfills can be an important source of renewable energy, we also designed a landfill gas extraction system. This system consisted of vertical gas extraction wells drilled into the waste, horizontal gas collectors, and a system of pipes to convey the gas to a nearby facility where the methane is burned to create electricity.

We drafted a set of design drawings, which were certified by a Professional Engineer (PE) before being reviewed by the state Department of Environmental Protection (DEP). After the DEP approved our design, we created a construction bid package, which included the design drawings, a list of all items required for the landfill cell construction, and technical specifications for the construction materials.

We also helped manage the cell construction. We held weekly meetings with the general contractor and geosynthetics installer, and one of our engineers stayed on site full-time to provide construction quality assurance. We reviewed the submittals from the contractor to make sure that all materials complied with our technical specifications. After the construction was completed, we worked with a Professional Land Surveyor to create a set of record drawings that showed everything constructed as part of the landfill cell. We submitted these drawings, along with a detailed construction certification report to the state DEP for review. When the DEP determined that the construction met the approved design, they issued an operating permit to allow waste disposal in the new cell. The entire process took about three years, from the initial environmental assessment to the operation of the first cell. It was very satisfying to see my design start out on paper and end up as a full-scale operating landfill cell.

-Katie Saltanovitz

One of the biggest problems that communities continually face is the effect of dumps on the environment, especially the drinking water, as substances in the dumps leach into the groundwater or stormwater.

Shop Talk: Denis Young

Denis Young is presently a teacher at Shenendehowa High School after 29 years as a civil engineer.

In 1993 I became the Project Engineer on a remedial landfill closure project that was estimated to cost over $35 million and take up to two years to finish. The landfill had been operated for over 100 years starting as a rural open dump. As the population of the local area grew, the location of the dump seemed to get closer to the residents of the city.

By the early 1980s the dump had evolved into a state permitted landfill of over 100 acres. By the late 1980s the closest (down-hill) homeowners had concerns about the quality of their drinking (well) water. The state environmental quality agency performed an environmental site investigation and found that industrial chemicals and wastes had found their way into the landfill during its operation.

The landfill was always operated as an unlined facility so the leakage/leaching of chemical contamination was expected. This fact forced a remedial investigation by the state environmental quality agency which generated the anticipated closure/clean-up cost estimate of $35 million.

The chosen remedial closure plan included relocating much of the waste/fill materials to lesson the final landfill footprint. The final remedial cover would be around 60 acres down from over 100+ acres. Storm water runoff would be collected and contained in a wetlands retention pond/reconstructed wetlands area and then the storm water flow would slowly travel into an adjacent stream.

The engineered remedial cover system would separate the annual precipitation events from the waste below, and thus stop the hydraulic push/ flushing of the landfill leachate (including the industrial chemistry) into the on site groundwater. This flushing had been occurring for many years at the uncovered landfill and had caused a groundwater quality concern for those down-gradient home-owners with (drinking water) wells. Alternate fill materials were used to help attain new surface grades.

Instead of using virgin soils to grade with, construction and demolition building materials were used, saving landfill volume at other permitted disposal sites, and saving material costs at this landfill project closure. A 6-mile waterline was installed to provide potable drinking water to the closest residents around the landfill that had down-gradient drinking water wells. The final closure cost for the project was under $11 million *a savings of $24 million not needed from the local, state, and federal taxpayers.*

- Denis Young

On the other end of controlling waste, efforts have to be made to keep sewage out of storm drains as much as possible, even in heavy rain. In the tech talk below, Rebecca Ducharme describes her role in "Keeping it Clean".

Shop Talk: Rebecca Ducharme

Rebecca Ducharme is an engineer at Tighe & Bond specializing in sewers and storm drainage. She is also very active in K-12 educational outreach and mentors a Future City Competition team in East Longmeadow, Massachusetts.

The design phase of the sewer separation project that the team and I are designing is almost complete. The project area involves an older neighborhood, which has flooding problems during and after heavy rain events. The street flooding and backups into resident's basements are caused by an undersized collection system. Unlike modern neighborhoods with designated sewer and storm drain systems, the combined system is unable to handle the additional flow from rain events.

The project will address problems with the current gravity system, such as the backups and will eliminate a sewer discharge outfall at the river edge. The storm drainage will be directed through a separate system to an outfall on the river. Many of the existing pipes will be TV Inspected and may later be used to transport storm drainage. The new separated sewer system will be installed parallel to the existing combined line to allow all of the houses and businesses access to a new separated sewer. All of the catch basins and any other sources of drainage will be connected to the designated storm drain system.

The design of a separated sewer system involves the development of specifications and contract drawings. The contract drawings show both plan and profile views of all of the new pipe runs. The majority of the calculations for this project involve determining the inverts in the manholes, checking the pipe clearance and determining pipe size. Existing utilities need to be carefully considered when designing the horizontal alignment of a sewer line. Details in the drawing show dimensions and material types for the proposed structures in the project. The pipes that are shown in profile view call out a material type, pipe size and slope for each pipe.

The project, as described by the contract drawings and specifications will then be advertised for bid and a contractor will be selected to install the new system. The engineer in charge of the project will *review the shop drawings to confirm that all of the materials meet the specifications.*

The construction phase of the project involves the installation of manholes and the sections of pipe in between the structures. During the construction phase a trench is dug and the pipeline is installed beginning at the downstream end. The pipe is bedded in crushed stone and the trench is backfilled and compacted. When installing the new system, the construction crew has to be aware of any existing utilities that may not be noted on the plans. Generally a construction observer will be assigned to the project to monitor the quality of the end product. It is very important that the materials used and the constructed project match what is indicated in the plans or the overall system may not work. Engineers make sure this happens.

-Rebecca Ducharme

Keeping water clean and properly handling wastewater are clearly efforts that are both critical to our survival on this planet and require considerable effort. While the topic is not always glamorous, there is something very cool about making the world a more livable place and saving lives.

Designing to Infinity and Beyond: Civil Engineers in Space

While in college, I had the unique opportunity to work with a professor that has had a great impact on me, Rick Johansen. He runs a company called E.T. Techtonics. Rick once worked for DuPont and was involved with using Kevlar in structural design. If you are unfamiliar with Kevlar, it is probably best known for its use in bullet-proof vests. In tension, Kevlar is five times stronger than steel. In its more basic form, it comes in clear strands similar to fiber optic cable (actually, Kevlar is useful as fiber optic cable), which can be made into ropes or combined into other materials to make very strong structural elements.

NASA (the space people) put out a request for proposals to design lightweight, strong structures that could be easily assembled in the space station without major equipment or large tools. Rick, along with others, proposed making structures out of fiber-reinforced polymer (putting high strength fibers into other plastics like fiberglass). They won the contract to develop and design structures for space deployment.

Rick left DuPont and became a structures professor at the University of Pennsylvania, where he did much of his research and testing. He started E.T. Techtonics in 1987, and I was lucky enough to be one of his students, who he let help him with the testing.

E.T. Techtonics does not currently mention its ties to space on its website. They do mention that they design and have manufactured lightweight, strong bridges out of fiber-reinforced plastic that can be easily installed. The site never mentions or suggests that the E.T. may stand for extra-terrestrial.

Rick's structural designs have been purchased by professional golf tours looking for structures that can pack into a small space, but quickly assembled to allow film crews and other staff to drive over course rough areas or wetlands without doing damage. He has made many bridges to span waterways on trails deep in the woods where standard construction equipment simply could not go. I worked with Rick a few years ago on such a project—in this case a bridge over a wetland in a state park.

There is a certain similarity between assembling a structure in space, in the middle of a golf course, or deep in the woods. In all cases, you need a lot of strength out of a little material. Also, it is hard to bring in heavy construction equipment without a major effort. There is one big difference between space and the woods: gravity.

I was recently invited to a school in Bath, Maine for "Space Day." I was asked to do an activity involving the design of structures in space. In space, the directions of loadings are not as simple as the downward forces we are accustomed to. Often, structures in space serve to hold things down. But what is "up" and what is "down"? The answers depend on the use of the structure and exactly where in space it will be put to use.

The environmental conditions of space structures are certainly different than those on terra firma. Space engineers must ask: Can the materials withstand the radiation they may be exposed to? What temperatures will the structure reach, and can the structure's materials handle them? What about the atmospheric pressure?

I do not want to get too philosophical about life in space, and future civilizations being formed out there. But I do want to make clear that in space, civil engineers are proudly going where no one has gone before.

Tying it all Together

Hopefully, you now have a good idea about what civil engineers do. You know what an engineer is. You know the many types of work that we civil engineers do.

When I asked members of the civil engineering community to write short descriptions of their work for students, the response was immediate and their words were very enthusiastic.

I was not surprised, I still find every day to be a new adventure, full of problems to solve and lives to better.

One letter I received was very different from the others.

In my experience as a civil engineer, I have found that civil engineers seem to have the flexibility to cross disciplines, perhaps more so than other engineering disciplines. This, I think, would be a great selling point to many young people who are deciding on a future career. I, for example, have done surveying, structural and civil design of bridges and highways and of buildings. I have also done field engineering and project management in construction. I ended up in the management of facilities for a Fortune 500 company for 25 years. All of this experience allowed me to do consulting as an owner's representative in building construction after I retired. Civil Engineering has been a rewarding and satisfying career for me and I have no hesitation in recommending life long careers in civil engineering to others.

-Bill Kennedy

Bill is not alone. I cannot count the number of civil engineers that just keep on keeping on, consulting and teaching well into their retirement years simply because they love what they do and they have so much to offer.

There is not fame or glory in civil engineering. Most people could not name two famous civil engineers. So, what is the allure that keeps a civil engineer wanting to continue even after retirement?

Like Bill says, a key ingredient is the variety of the work. You can work outdoors, or you can chain yourself to a computer. You can entrench yourself in intense analysis, or spend your time talking to a community to assure their satisfaction and approval. The work is never too backbreaking, and never too dull. But this alone is not "it."

Perhaps the "it" has something to do with the visible improvements that result from our efforts, or how you can feel yourself gaining knowledge every passing year.

I have heard civil engineering referred to as the "noblest of the engineering professions." Some civil engineers have adopted it as a moniker for their profession, and there is a good deal to support such a bold statement. Some refer to themselves as "stewards of the infrastructure," and claim that civil engineering profession improves the lives of people, more even than doctors. Others are less high and mighty.

There are all types of people in this field, and because the nature of the work is so grounded in what many take for granted, there are strong forces acting to keep snobbery to a minimum.

There is a certain pride that flows with the civil engineering field, and how best to capture it than in a verse by Rudyard Kipling of Jungle Book and Rikki Tikki Tavi fame.

When you read this poem (slightly trimmed), entitled "Sons of Martha", think of "Civil Engineers" as the "Sons of Martha", and when you read "Sons of Mary" think of the public.

"...the Sons of Martha... They say to mountains, "Be ye removed" They say to the lesser floods "Be dry."
Under their rods are the rocks reproved - they are not afraid of that which is high.
Then do the hill-tops shake to the summit - then is the bed of the deep laid bare,
That the Sons of Mary may overcome it, pleasantly sleeping and unaware.

*To these from birth is Belief forbidden; from these till
death is Relief afar.
They are concerned with matters hidden - under the
earthline their altars are:
The secret fountains to follow up, waters withdrawn to
restore to the mouth,
And gather the floods as in a cup, and pour them
again at a city's drouth.*

*They do not preach that their God will rouse them a
little before the nuts work loose.
They do not teach that His Pity allows them to leave
their job when they damn-well choose.
As in the thronged and the lighted ways, so in the dark
and the desert they stand,
Wary and watchful all their days that their brethren's
days may be long in the land.*

*Raise ye the stone or cleave the wood to make a path
more fair or flat;
Lo, it is black already with blood some Son of Martha
spilled for that!
Not as a ladder from earth to Heaven, not as a witness
to any creed,
But simple service simply given to his own kind in their
common need..."*

Rudyard Kipling wrote this poem to be part of
a ceremony for graduating engineers in Canada
(The Ritual of the Calling of the Engineer). There,
new graduates are given a ring of either iron or
steel after making a solemn statement of pure
ethical intent, to wear on the pinky of their writing
hand that will touch all future works.

I participated in the U.S. ceremony known as "The Order of the Engineer" and proudly wear the ring. It is a truly beautiful tradition. In this ceremony, engineers, not necessarily recently graduating, state the "Obligation of the Engineer"

I am an engineer, in my profession I take deep pride. To it I owe solemn obligations. Since the stone age, human progress has been spurred by the engineering genius. Engineers have made usable, nature's vast resources of material and energy for humanity's benefit. Engineers have vitalized and turned to practical use the principles of science and the means of technology. Were it not for this heritage of accumulated experience, my efforts would be feeble. As an engineer, I pledge to practice integrity and fair dealing, tolerance, and respect and to uphold devotion to the standards and the dignity of my profession, conscious always that my skill carries with it the obligation to serve humanity by making the best use of earth's precious wealth. As an engineer, I shall participate in none but honest enterprises. When needed, my skill and knowledge shall be given without reservation for the public good. In the performance of duty and in fidelity to my profession, I shall give the utmost.

-Rudyard Kipling

In parts of the world like Iraq and Dubai, civil engineers seem to be looked up to like the Romans or Egyptians looked up to the great "master builders." So if the field is so wonderful, why does the world hear so little about it? Where are the civil engineering superheroes? Where are the TV shows and movies about great civil engineers? Sometimes, the best answer is simply "who cares?" Civil engineers often keep out of the public view, but this behind-the-scenes role does not diminish the effect of their work for the community, and the overall satisfaction of those working in the field.

The civil engineers know the significance of their work. The positive effect of any project was already researched, brainstormed, and detailed out long before the project comes to life. We envision it. We make it happen.

"Civil How?!": How to Get Hands-On with Civil Engineering before College

The nice thing about the world of civil engineering is that your everyday world IS the civil engineering world. You don't really need to look very far to see a project created by a civil engineer and most hands-on activities involving civil engineering require everyday materials. And there is a great civil engineering project, activity, or contest waiting for you, no matter what grade you're in (check out www.engineeryourfuture.org).

Many hands-on community service projects are civil engineering projects. Get involved! Groups like Rebuilding Together, Habitat for Humanity, and Engineers Without Borders do not require a degree for volunteers and they would welcome you with open arms. Wherever you are, there is likely to be something going on nearby you can take part in.

Paid work is sometimes tougher for a high-school student to come by, but there are many engineers out there happy to spend some time with someone asking to learn, especially if a student just wants to tag along and not prevent them from getting their work done.

Some schools are working civil engineering right into the curriculum. In Massachusetts, engineering was given its own place in the educational requirements alongside math, science, English and social studies. I have been meeting once a week to help develop engineering activities for a Boston school, and have worked with many teachers developing similar units.

Engineering is best learned hands-on. Museums, colleges, and professional organizations regularly have activity days. There is a website www.mydiscover-e.org that was created as a posting place for such activities. Check it out. If you know of activities that are not listed on the site, tell the organizer about it.

Another source is the website pbskids.org. On the PBS website, whether you look at Design Squad Nation, Fetch! With Ruff Ruffman, Curious George, or Zoom, you can find directions for hands-on activities by clicking on the "Parents and Teachers" link. Another of my favorite sources for activities is www.worldwatermonitoringday.org.

I am involved with "ThinkFest", an event held at Merrimack College where high school juniors and seniors build catapults and compete for a scholarship (technically, it is a trebuchet competition, but that's a discussion for a mechanical engineering book). The competition is followed by a free event for the public where over a dozen design challenges are set up and students of all ages collect prizes for designing better solutions.

At Construction Career Days, busloads of students are brought to get experience with construction equipment, and solve design challenges to win school prizes. Somewhere near you, something is happening as well.

There are many civil engineers out there that visit schools or guide field trips regularly, myself being one of them. Instead of taking another trip to a museum, get a civil engineer to show you a project for a couple hours. At this point there is no simple system for finding these engineers, but there are people in engineering societies like ASCE that would be happy to help steer you in the right direction, so do not hesitate to contact outreach@asce.org for assistance.

"Civil Me!": How to Become Part of the Civil Engineering World

"There is more than one way to skin a cat." Although this old expression conjures a disturbing image, it is something to keep in mind if you are thinking about becoming a civil engineer.

In the civil engineering world, there are both civil engineers who pursue formal college education and then licensure, and civil engineering technologists who take a different road.

I have heard many times that an engineer needs a minimum of a 4-year engineering degree, and soon will need a Master's degree but I have seen people take all sorts of paths to become a civil engineer. Some of my friends have taken very roundabout paths. One of them had little interest in college at first, he liked hunting and flying planes. He moved to Alaska, flew planes, and led hunting expeditions. He got into surveying while up there. Only then did he go back to school for a degree, and he gained interest in civil engineering through his interest in surveying. (You do not typically get a four-year degree in surveying, but in many civil engineering programs you learn surveying as part of the curriculum.)

A surveyor is considered one type of engineering technologist. Never look at the role of an engineering technologist as being something inferior to an engineer, even though there is connection between salary, level of responsibility at a company, and education level. I have met many brilliant surveyors, and surveyors also need to become licensed if they want to take responsibility in their work. Some surveyors can also make salaries comparable to an engineer, and many do have higher degrees. Many survey because they enjoy surveying.

You do not need to jump into a 4-year engineering program. I have seen many engineers start out at a 2-year community college, and often have several years of work in unrelated fields. Traditional engineering programs are not cheap, and your life situation may not really lead to a 4-year program after high school. Also, like many young people, you may not be quite sure what you want to do, and want a better sense of your goals before entering into a costly program.

How costly is an engineering program, anyway? Although tuition can be up to $50,000 per year at some schools, others are far less expensive, and financial aid and scholarships may be available. Spend the time to figure this out if you cannot afford tuition. Talk to guidance counselors, read books, visit the College Board website. Research local scholarships. You have nothing to lose except a little expended effort in doing this research, and a whole lot to gain. If you want to be a civil engineer, do not let financial aspects deter you.

And do not believe the myth about engineering being for only those who love math and science.

I was recently reading a brochure about engineering put out by National Engineers Week that read "Math is the basis of engineering, but you don't have to love it. You just have to be able to do it." I remember this quote well because I mulled it over in my head for much of a long plane trip. A very different quote that I hold as a basic life principle is "Do what you love, and you will never need to work a day in your life." This quote about math seemed to say something different.

Then it hit me: math is not the basis of engineering. Solving problems may be deep in the roots of engineering, but that is not necessarily math. But then I remembered college when I did an awful lot of calculations on the way to my degree. And then I remembered the professional engineering licensure exam, and how entrenched in math that was. Do I love math? I certainly do not hate it, but LOVE? I don't know.

When new recruits go to boot camp, the odds are slim that they will love it, but they need to learn the skills necessary to do work that they might love later. Some college courses you may really enjoy, and some will be more challenging. Regardless, you DO need to be able to learn math.

A mathematician better love mathematics. A scientist better love scientific research. And engineers better enjoy solving problems using their whole body of knowledge, which includes scientific principles, mathematics, an understanding of civics, sociology and laws, a boatload of good old-fashioned logic, and much more. Nowhere is there a rule that you should love learning everything in your bag of tricks, you just need to enjoy finding answers in the bag in your brain to solve a problem when the time is right. If you keep in mind that everything you learn may come in use, that it may someday have some real practical application for you, and it may help you in swallowing some of the toughest concepts.

Do not let a subject matter scare you. Get into whatever you are doing. Talk about the topics with your classmates. Get to know your professors and ask them questions. Get to feel that the subject is important to you.

In most civil engineering schools, there is opportunity to get involved with extra-curricular activities that are perfect for reminding you why you are taking all of these courses. Many schools enter the ASCE Steel Bridge Competition and the Concrete Canoe Competition. (Yes, design a canoe out of concrete and race it.) These programs can give you not only the chance to do something exciting, but also a growing bag of tricks, and experience conquering challenges.

The choice of school is very personal, and one that is ranked higher or is more popular may not be what you are looking for.

Remember that many engineers start out as

technologists: cost estimators, CAD technicians, survey crew members and many others, have a change of heart, go back to school a little later in life. Many engineers get their degrees in part-time programs, often with the bulk of their courses at night.

There is a broad range of colleges out there and a student looking for a career in civil engineering can take as traditional or nontraditional a path as he or she chooses. There may be challenges along the way. Some days will be fun and exciting, other days will be plain old hard work, but that is the way life is. In my humble opinion, a life spent working hard as a civil engineer is a life well lived.

The following is one last bit of shop talk before we end this book, this time from a civil engineering student in his final year of college.

Shop Talk: Rich Matson

Rich Matson is a senior at Merrimack College. Along his path there, he met and overcame many obstacles, and has had to work very hard along the way. Rich was my co-op last year, and he has inspired me, just as I hope that I have inspired him. Rich

is not some sort of child prodigy; he is simply someone who wants to do what he enjoys.

As the first in my family to ever attend college, I have been faced with many new and difficult challenges. My father successfully owned and operated a sign company for over 20 years before claiming bankruptcy in 2004. I was only a junior in high school and needed to work three jobs to help support my family. I knew this wasn't the life for me and I needed to find something to change my life.

I was always good at math and science and wanted to pursue a career in that field. Unfortunately, my high school never taught me about engineering as, at the time, only calculus, chemistry and physics courses were offered. I looked around and found out about the Summer Transportation Institute (STI) program at Merrimack College, applied and was accepted into this program during the summer of 2005. This program exposes high school students to career opportunities in transportation through seminars, hands-on laboratories, field trips and team building activities. Another benefit to this four-week program is it is 100% free. My family surely would not have the means to pay for a summer engineering camp, so this was the perfect fit for me.

Upon completion of this STI program, I was awarded the "Best Future Engineer Award." I was encouraged by my peers to apply for a Bachelor of Science in Civil Engineering and attend a four-year college or university. My grades in high school were certainly not perfect as I only had a GPA of 2.8, but with my extracurricular activities such as playing in varsity sports and working three jobs to survive, I was not discouraged to apply to college. In fact, I was motivated to prove others wrong by receiving my early acceptance into Merrimack College and three other universities.

As my family was in the process of starting over by moving to South Carolina my senior year, I was given the option to co-own the business with my father or put myself through college. I chose the more challenging path and worked my way through high school and accepted an offer at Merrimack College to study civil engineering.

I chose the Merrimack College civil engineering program largely because of STI and wanted to give other high school students the same opportunity I had by joining the program as a counselor. I offered advice and encouraged over 50 students to pursue a college degree through three years as a counselor for STI.

I have been able to successfully fund my entire education at Merrimack College through work, scholarships and loans. Unfortunately, my parents are unable to provide the funds needed to attend college, as they have their own financial struggles. I really want to stress how important it is to have a good credit history. As most teenagers and young adults don't think about their finances too much, you never know when your financial situation will change. When my parents went bankrupt, it ruined their credit history and therefore they could not co-sign a student loan. Since I had a credit card and always made my payments on time, I had enough credit to sign my own student loans. This would not be possible if it was not for early planning in high school.

As many college students like to go out on the weekends, my situation has been a bit different. I have held a weekend job for about six years now as a server. I have worked just about every Friday, Saturday and Sunday throughout my entire college career. It surely has not been easy at times, especially early on in the first couple of years, but I had to find a balance in my life to get by. My will to succeed and never give up attitude is what keeps me going and is a necessity for my survival.

Another unique thing about Merrimack College is the co-op program. I strongly encourage all students who have the opportunity to participate in a co-op program to do so. With co-op I was able to work in two engineering firms and gain valuable experience. It may take five years to graduate, but trust me, that extra year goes by so quickly and is worth the benefits of having work experience. Also, it was another opportunity for me to earn some extra money to reduce my student loans needed to pay for tuition.

With all that said, my life has guided me in a direction full of opportunity. I will never stop learning. In fact I feel my day is not complete *until I learn something new and make someone smile. I am on track to finish up with my Bachelor of Science degree in civil engineering with a minor in mathematics at Merrimack College in May 2011. I have applied to Tufts University and look to excel in a Master of Science degree in Structural Engineering starting in the Fall of 2011. My advice to you is to never stop following your dreams. Don't settle for anything less. It will be difficult and will take a lot of hard work and perseverance, but if you overcome adversity, never give up, and keep fighting for what you want, you will succeed!*

I will leave you with one quote that has inspired me which I heard from a fellow engineer, Larry Smith, who said "the nicest thing about the hard road is that there is no traffic!"

-Rich Matson

Not everybody needs to take the hard road like Rich, but everyone should choose a path that takes them where they want to go, and always remember to enjoy both the path and the scenery along the way. There is an infinite number of paths. Naturally, not everyone will want to be a civil engineer, but it is the sincere hope of this author that a little light has been shed on the field of civil engineering and the people behind our infrastructure. And remember, whatever path you do take, there is probably a civil engineer somewhere making it safer and smoother for you.

About the Author

Reed Brockman is a Senior Structural Engineer and Inspection Specialist in Boston, for AECOM, a large engineering company who is very patient with his obsession about pre-college engineering education. At the time of this press release, Reed is the Senior Vice President of the Boston Society of Civil Engineers (BSCES), a section of the American Society of Civil Engineers (ASCE) that started in the mid-1800's. He is past-chair of their Infrastructure Technical Group and the longtime standing chair of its Committee of Pre-College Outreach. He regularly makes presentations at schools, runs and designs activities with them, and takes them on field trips. He is co-founder of ThinkFest, founder of the Ralph Salvucci Online Bridge Design Contest (which is a local contest within the West Point Bridge Design Contest), and he is the New England Regional Coordinator for the Future City Competition. He is also on the ASCE Committee on Volunteer Community Service and the ASCE Committee on Pre-College Outreach. ASCE has presented him with the Edmund Freeman Award for Professional Recognition and the BSCES has given him the Citizen Engineer Award and its President's Award. The outreach program he runs through the BSCES has received numerous awards over the past decade for both outstanding public service and its diversity efforts. Mr. Brockman is also a board member of the DOME Foundation and the Metro-North Regional Employment Board, and has participated in numerous panels promoting STEM (Science, Technology, Engineering and Mathematics) education in schools. Really, Reed is a big kid, and he is very grateful that his wife, Larisa, puts up with his constant involvement in schools. He has three kids, one big and two still little, as well as fish, frogs and a very loud cockatiel. He grew up as a big fan of "Games" magazine. There may or may not be hidden contests in this book.

Other Engineering Career Publications from the Engineering Education Service Center

The Musical Engineer: A Music Enthusiast's Guide to Engineering and Technology Careers. $17.95

The Maritime Engineer: A Music Enthusiast's Guide to Engineering and Technology Careers. $17.95

The Fantastical Engineer: A Thrillseeker's Guide to Careers in Theme Park Engineering. $17.95

High Tech Hot Shots: Careers in Sports Engineering. $19.95

Is There an Engineer Inside You? A Comprehensive Guide to Career Decisions in Engineering. $29.95

Ideas in Action: A Girl's Guide to Careers in Engineering $7.95

To Order:
call 1-360-341-1424
Fax orders to 1-360-341-1434
Online orders www.engineeringedu.com

 Engineering Education Service Center